THE FORGIVENESS PROJECT

A MEMOIR:
Reclaiming My Narrative

MEKA RUSE, EDD

WESTBOW
PRESS®
A DIVISION OF THOMAS NELSON
& ZONDERVAN

WestBow Press books may be ordered through booksellers or by contacting:

WestBow Press
A Division of Thomas Nelson & Zondervan
1663 Liberty Drive
Bloomington, IN 47403
www.westbowpress.com
844-714-3454

ISBN: 979-8-3850-0464-5 (sc)
ISBN: 979-8-3850-0465-2 (e)

Library of Congress Control Number: 2023915441

Print information available on the last page.

WestBow Press rev. date: 8/22/2023

For learning about wisdom and instruction, for understanding words of insight, for gaining instruction in wise dealing, righteousness, justice, and equity; to teach shrewdness to the simple, knowledge and prudence to the young – let the wise also hear and gain in learning, and the discerning acquire skill to understand a proverb and a figure, the words of the wise and their riddles. Proverbs 1:2-6 (NRSV)

CONTENTS

PROLOGUE

The Forgiveness Project is an invitation to lean into reconciliation. Walk alongside me through snippets of who I was and whom forgiveness allows me to become. Then, launch into your current reality with an openness to the spirit of grace and mercy cultivated in the private grip of acts of forgiveness. Here we can safely unpack our inner satchels, which are full to overflowing with grief and the toxicity of our pain and hurt. Pain kindled in tracing past moments that have, without question, affected our lived experience. A dose of targeted forgiveness yields a promising future as it opens the opportunity for deeper meditative liturgical inspiration.

Wrestling with those formative years in our rearview mirror can be like standing on top of a mountain gazing into a valley covered with trees. We notice various stages of development in treetops and attempt to diagnose their nutritional needs. We use our imperfect scale to set variations in their shades of green and size as facts of stunted growth. Formerly drawing parallels to your own life while questioning its lack of robustness can also be an art form. What is a true measure of worth? Is it a failure of one's life to add value to societal needs? Acts of forgiveness are personal ventures that fastens us to the forest floor. Here, I often lose the holistic view of the forest because there are so many unique trees responding to me. Psalm 1 places these trees next to waters, offering nourishment as advice to the delight of the Lord. What will the outcome of proper spiritual watering be when we seek ways to remain fruitful, abiding next to God's still waters?

Self-doubt is such a universal thread in many of our psyches. Reveling in one's conversation with "self" can become yet another process that helps some reseed their own forest. The Forgiveness Project gave me a process to harvest the good, clear the impure, and replant the narrative of my soul, replacing trees that had, over time, succumbed to hurricane-force winds. I let the memories in my head flow through me, displaying scars like marks etched into tree trunks. Reflecting on my childhood while feeling overwhelmed has helped me assess things with a new perspective now that I'm older.

There were two significant circumstances that affected my childhood community. First, fewer and inadequate schools made life for students in my community challenging during the 1950s. Discrimination, sexism, and racism meant that teachers could only teach certain subjects.[1]

> The number-one issue involving education in the United States during the 1950s was school integration. For decades, qualified black Americans had been denied admission to whites-only colleges and public schools. Additionally, the "separate but equal" doctrine, as outlined by the U.S. Supreme Court in the *Plessy* v. *Ferguson* case of 1896, had long been the basis for segregating whites and blacks in public schools. "Separate but equal" meant that blacks and whites could attend separate schools and thereby receive equal opportunities for education. However, particularly in the South, the schools attended by white children were more modern and better equipped to support extracurricular subjects beyond basic Reading, Writing and Math.[2]

---

[1] https://www.bartleby.com/essay/School-Life-in-the-1950s-FK2LBE936YZA
[2] The 1950s Education: Overview | Encyclopedia.com

Secondly, the post-war framing of my family's access to resources was the Servicemen's Readjustment Act, known by many as the G.I. Bill. This bill funded hospitals, gave veterans low-interest mortgages, and provided college or trade school tuition. Family members, like my father and uncles, were among the many World War II veterans denied these pivotal federal benefits. And therefore—

> When lawmakers began drafting the G.I. Bill in 1944, some Southern Democrats feared that returning Black veterans would use public sympathy for veterans to advocate against Jim Crow laws. John Rankin, Mississippi's congressional representative, insisted that individual states administer the program instead of the federal government. This made sure the G.I. Bill largely benefited white people. The southern Democrats drew on tactics they had previously used to ensure that the New Deal helped as few Black people as possible. In 1947, only 2 of the over 3,200 VA-guaranteed home loans in 13 Mississippi cities went to Black borrowers. "They did not confine these impediments to the South," notes historian Ira Katznelson. "In New York and the northern New Jersey suburbs, fewer than 100 of the 67,000 mortgages insured by the G.I. bill supported home purchases by non-whites." As the years went on, White veterans flowed into newly created suburbs, where they began amassing wealth in skilled positions. But Black veterans lacked those options. They gave the most skilled jobs to White workers too.

My childhood family setting was a small town in the northeast corner of Mississippi. A town of 17,000 during the 1950s. Our post-World War II southern neighborhood might differ from that of your own. Corporal punishment gave way to spankings being commonly enforced by teachers and parents in our cultural isolation.

This punishment style had Mississippi State law support for these tactics in both our home and school settings.

I can't talk about my historic journey without drawing upon interactions between myself and close relatives. It is within this context that I will cast aside this cloak of shame tossed on my shoulders by them and others. With this personal mindfulness comes an obligation to alter the names of the main characters. This respects and offers privacy to family members, their offspring, and friends who continue their journey among us.

Characters: The narrator disputes any positive or negative correlation about any specific relationship. These character names and titles are pseudonyms –

Tassey – paternal grandmother Jasmine & Evette – paternal aunts	Linda – Mama Carrie Lou – maternal great aunt Nana, Sally Ann – maternal grandmother March - maternal aunt
Meka's siblings – David, Mandy, Rufus, Candy Meka's 35+ year marriage partner - Theodis	

While exploring my adverse reactions to high-stress situations many years later, I pondered reasons "why I reacted in subdued mannerism to life's stresses." There could be a link between my early exposure to unresolved trauma and setting unhealthy boundaries. Pain experienced from years of embarrassment created a drip, drip, drip of emotions like lemon juice into a thimble, supporting my cause for unforgiveness. Might this understanding have a major influence on my life, both personal and public?

My sporadic emotional drip became a steady stream that revealed a deep bitterness fueled by hurt feelings. I finally recognized and owned my need to assess forgiveness and its role as a spiritual discipline at a deeper and more personal level. This Forgiveness

Project is my approach to examining my bouts with humiliation and embarrassment and how I processed them. This is my journey to becoming more grateful for my God-ordained raw experiences and the narrative they created.

SHAME AND TRAUMA

The Lord helps me; therefore, I have not been disgraced;
therefore, I have set my face like flint, and I know I shall
not be put to shame; he who vindicates me is near.
—Isaiah 50:7 (NRSV)

Do I feel angry, or is it shame dressed in humiliation, being credited
with keeping me emotionally detached from those I want to assist?
Or those I'm called to love? Are these the primary emotions I conjure
up when I reflect on early childhood and my life's journey? Or might
embarrassment or humiliation play a role? All rendition of myself is
inviting the world into my domain as we attempt to dismantle walls
constructed of social bricks molded in the past. We've carried the
weight of this wall in response to these and other questions about
relations. Do we stand alone or stand among others who have given
a place of power to opposing forces throughout their life?

"One reason shame is so powerful is its
ability to make us feel alone."
– Brene Brown, Ph.D., LMSW

Spiritual gloominess regularly encounters latent trauma. When
colleagues leave an opening for my voice during informal conversations
about life, I'm awkwardly silent. Thus, this reflection on life is both
a primer and a witness to my commitment to prioritize forgiveness.

It's a life-changing ride down bumpy roads to paths filled with encouragement for all willing to enter. The rationale for actions taken by core family members over the course of a lifetime can place younger relatives in a crippling downdraft. Those of us willing to accept never knowing or understanding details of "the whys" from our childhood clearly must find solace. Hurtful attitudes in future generations can stem from unclear adult decisions.

It's the curiosity about my reluctance to talk about myself even when people are spreading incorrect information set me to wondering "why?"

Shame always accompanied childhood memories of poor housing, clothing, and family. People I looked up to were seeding unhealthy ideas about social status. A tone set for how Mama's offspring would ostracize us seemed to gain traction years before our birth. People in our small community were saying mean things about Mama, and it made the other kids, and their parents think it was okay to be rude to us as well. The never-ending core narrative bruised my siblings and me for our foreseeable future. Feeling like damaged goods, without family interventions like counseling, brings us to a spiritual pause. Our story predates the discovery by sociologists that bullying and shaming are dangerous to one's well-being.

My early exposure to bullying led to rogue thoughts. They followed me like villains. They occupied space in my mind's eye, right through my adulthood into professional and private life. Core supporters provided food and clothing. This helped disguise their tactics as aides. Reality placed their parenting approach essential to me establishing an unhealthy low-self-esteem lifestyle.

Self-anger was the binding force that owned my code of silence; the need to be accepted, and the longing to be appreciated. Feelings of shamefulness always expanding and retracting, like blowing on embers to kindle a fire. The air made glowing embers spark into captivating tall tales about me from people I knew. They joyfully complemented the stories my core caregivers and acquaintances told.

"You are an ugly, dark-skinned social embarrassment," close relatives often told me. The hurt carried within led to many years of never striving to push beyond the narrative that made accommodating others rise to unhealthy levels. I became the leading critic. Nevertheless, after working closely with troubled and neglected youth in the Safe Haven Afterschool Outreach, God's grace kindled a curiosity about my own personal experiences. How might forgiveness play a role in reclaiming or recreating a wholesome narrative? Could a sense of dignity improve and sweeten the sour demeanor of my childhood journey? The Forgiveness Project seeks to stir up an appreciation for others that spills over and touches the lives of other adults. People who view their experiences as obstacles rather than learning opportunities could benefit from an inventory of forgiveness. You will find a mixture of painful and humorous snippets throughout this book to help get us started. Add your own to the book margins in response to your ponderings as this project unfolds.

> Do you hoard any codes of silences? Share one.

I wholeheartedly accredit my training as clergy to kindling fire for another approach to looking at forgiveness. This desire to probe and dig into the chambers of my own spiritual existence and take on a thorough unpacking of forgiveness, again. This God inspired quest needs to move not only beyond the work of our beloved theologian duties but also into a personal spirituality of our own rumblings. My pivotal moments hang on *The Book on Forgiving* by Desmond Tutu *and* Mpho Tutu; and *Convicted: A Crooked Cop* by Jameel Zookie McGee, Andrew Collins, Mark Tabb after their presentation at a police reform function in Cleveland, Ohio. Their work chronicled the path of an innocent man, and an unlikely journey to forgiveness and friendship. Reading about their breakthrough put me on a path to reviewing other non-cleric work like - *The Guide to Compassionate Assertiveness: How to Express Your Needs & Deal with Conflict While*

Keeping a Kind Heart by Sherrie M. Vavrichek, LCSW-C; *The Gratitude Power Workbook: Transform Fear into Forgiveness, Isolation into Belonging* (2011) by Nina Lesowitz and Mary Beth Sammons; and *Taking Out Your Emotional Trash* (2010) by Georgia Shaffer. This list represents a few resources that lead to my initial title selection, *The Forgiveness Project: How's that working for You?* for this work. These resources moved me to use a podcast format at the initiation of my project. It served as a mechanism to help me commit to processing forgiveness beyond my general religious and sometimes rote understanding. The podcast started January 2020 is still available. The genre held me accountable for living into forgiveness as a discipline, while I sought to pry open the calloused effect on my early childhood. Unpacking my own fears and struggles against

> Let us forgive one another and walk toward reconciliation. Happy times; sad times; in between times; GOD uses them all as GOOD TIMES. Likewise, the Spirit helps us in our weakness; for we do not know how to pray as we ought, but that every Spirit intercedes with sights too deep for words. And God, who searches the heart, knows what the mind of the Spirit is because the Spirit intercedes for the saints according to the will of God. We know all things work together for good for those who love God, who are called according to his purpose.
> **Romans 8:26-28 (NRSV)**

thoughts, craving family support beyond a place to live and clothes to wear. Emotional care was lacking and never discussed. With this writing, I'm seeking a path supported by the authority of God's grace and mercy. One where forgiveness thoroughly teaches us to let go of our own imperfections and the imperfections of others. These opposing poles of thought must learn to co-exist as we way fare to the other side of painful encounters. Learning to raise a standard that teaches us to embrace gratefulness for a journey salty enough to yield a flavorful taste of God's goodness.

INFLUENCERS: MEETING OUR OUTSIDE AND INSIDE VOICES

My core family included Mama, a stepfather, and four younger siblings [David (age three), Mandy (age two), Rufus (age two) and Candy (age one)], and me (four). During our early years, we spent most days playing in the yard. Jacks, Marbles, Paper Dolls, and Hide n' Seek were our favorite pastime games when making mud pies as make-believe food didn't energize us.

Miss Latham, the landlord, and her father occupied most of the rooms in the house where our family lived. Our kitchen was a standalone one-room structure right behind the main house. It was available for use by both families. Our family rented a large room for our living quarters, which was really three rooms in one. This space was a shelter on rainy days, used for sleeping, eating, and social time.

I am from the generation of children whose parents disciplined them with that "parenting LOOK" method. Mama's parenting look was a raised brow with an eye roll and tight lips. "Don't any of you go over there into Miss Latham's living space without being invited!" I remember Mama often saying to us as she shook her index finger of one hand at us while her other hand rested on her waist. Mama was uncompromising with us about adhering to the rules of the house! We had to learn through spoken and non-verbal cues, which required us to guess a lot about what behavior adults wanted or expected from us.

Setting limits was a vital resource in my mother's parenting repertoire. Years later, researchers have learned that parents' behaviors in those early years are the best influencers of a child's personal-social formation. Studies emphasize respect for oneself and others, and language development is influenced by parents' behaviors in a child's early years. I often wonder how their discipline style affected the growth of my self-confidence, understanding, hearing, speaking abilities, and overall resiliency.

We didn't live close to a natural stream or river. But, on summer days after heavy rainfall, the neighborhood block we lived on would flood and transform into a makeshift swimming hole. Let's be clear: The neighborhood swimming hole came alive after heavy summer rains because of poor drainage. Our parents would let us play in the muddy water and laugh as we attempted to mimic the arm motions of swimmers we had seen in movies or read about in books. I remember there came a time when we were still quite young Mama banned the practice. The water we swam in may have had sewage and rainwater pollution.

As small children, we never spent a day without meals. We gathered around a newspaper spread on the floor. Mama served us home-cooked meals in the corner of our large room. Sometimes, our feet touch slightly, creating an octagon-shaped border like a protected tabletop. I was not too fond of it when Mama served us overcooked black-eyed peas. Those tiny worm-like things floating around in the broth gave the meal an unpleasant visual appearance. Later learnings identified those unpleasant-looking floaters as the "eyes" from the overcooked black-eyed peas. I refused to eat those worms. There was no compromise from either one of us.

Other living space-shaping objects were a full-size bed, a refrigerator, a four-drawer dresser with a mirror, and a roll-away bed. Three siblings slept in the same roll-away bed with me, and Candy slept at the foot of Mama and Daddy's bed. A pot-belly wood heater, set in the center of the room, belonged to the landlord. We did not have a table or chairs. I fondly remember eating meals with my siblings while sitting on the floor. Memories of dining with them in this fashion still make me smile. We thought this was the way all young children ate their meals.

Making a pallet during summer evenings to sleep on the floor fit right in with our informal lifestyle (a description I would later learn). Every action required Mama's approval. One funny incident about a warm Mississippi summer night comes to mind. It happened when I was approximately four years old. Mama had permitted us to sleep on the floor. She was not in the room overseeing our final tuck in that night. On this particular night, the bright idea was to sleep in our play clothes. Sleeping on the floor was a treat and doing it in play clothes seemed like a logical, efficient next step. Waking up already dressed for a full day of play would put us ahead with daily chores—more time to play with friends the next day. My siblings did not grasp the genius spunk of this idea. Therefore, with help from that inner voice, approval was not a problem. I explored it on my own for immediate use.

As a side note, yelling still causes me to enter a mental freeze zone! It renders me, ultimately, momentarily non-functional; it causes an emotional standstill.

The following day, Mama didn't see the wittiness of my decision. She did not even see it as a humorous act. "Brainless and lazy girl!" was my Mama's morning shower of words voicing her disapproval. Her trademark yelling and use of degrading labels were helpful reminders never to repeat the idea. Her harsh verbal reaction made my feelings of insecurity and low self-worth resurface. Feelings I had struggled with at other times at the young age of three or four.

Yelling at me still causes me to enter a mental freeze zone! It renders me, ultimately, momentarily non-functional; it causes an emotional standstill. Have you noticed any carry-over non-verbal responses from your childhood?

NAUGHTINESS OR
SEARCHING FOR PLACE?

Let me tell you about when I helped myself to watermelon meant for the whole family. Picture this: all of us, the kids, both Mama and stepdad, are outside hoping to catch a cool summer breeze on this smoldering Mississippi day. While the adults sat on the front porch in the shade, kids from the neighborhood played an exhausting game of hide' n' seek. They were running and romping around the house's perimeter, racing from the front-to-back yard and then back again. Consuming this much energy running for the fun of it made us thirsty. Our parents encouraged us to take quick breaks. Mama was fine with our friends and us getting a cold drink of water from the refrigerator without adult supervision during playtime.

This unsupervised privilege was ideal. So, darting through the front door and into the fridge with some frequency for a cold drink did not raise concerns. These eyes of mine focused on a yummy watermelon on one of the water breaks. It was half of a large, round red meat watermelon. Cutting a tiny piece from the center probably will not be noticed. Hmmm, yummy – it was so refreshing and juicy and sweet.

Personal trips for water increased. Each refrigerator sashay included a sip of water and another small piece of watermelon. There were only a few small but deep digs at each stop. I ate only half of the entire half, most of the tasty, sweet center section. Breaks were enhanced by a tiny, delicious teaspoon scoop at a time, without Mama's blessings or knowing.

One parent, our stepfather, was paying close attention to everyone's comings and goings, and he informed Mama. Exercising this freedom ended when the watermelon half had a noticeable missing center. Like any kid, I quickly wondered who knew and told the tale about the secret treat added to getting water. How did they know it was not a neighbor kid?

Looking back on a parent role, the increased frequency of getting water raised his curiosity. Like any adult, he saw what happened during those frequent trips to get water. Nothing physical happened like a spanking this time. However, worst of all, Mama was a master at punishment by yelling and name-calling, adult intimidation, and bullying by any definition.

"Girl, you know you know better! Get your rear end in the house." Mama yelled. There were many lingering memories and childhood moments like this one from a hot summer Mississippi day when I was six.

Parenting in my environment did not include words of guidance for the long term.

Rays of compassion didn't trickle down upon us from the adults in our lives. Only names of shame and the accompanying feelings of rejection. This adult posture would become commonplace to me at an early age rather than expressions of love and happiness. These realities of everyday life were another step into my abyss of loneliness and feelings of confusion.

Appointed adult caregivers used degrading yelling and corporal punishment to correct their children's misbehavior. Yes, real spankings or slaps across the face were acceptable parenting practices during the 1950s and 60s. Moreover, Mama issued plenty of those during our childhood.

Times when Mama lovingly hugged us or made us feel like essential members of the family seemed minimal during childhood. Sadly, we never bonded with aunts, uncles, or godparents as confidants to ask for guidance during those years. Playing board games or card games with maternal grandparents or any adult was nonexistent as part of our informal learning and social-emotional development.

Waking up after being hit in the head with a poke iron remains on the list of childhood traumas scarred over. Asking for help with schoolwork at home invoked fear of being yelled at if the concept wasn't grasped quickly. I remember feeling like my thoughts, needs, or opinions were unimportant to others. It would be years beyond early childhood before these reflections mattered. Are these reflections descriptions of childhood trauma?

While some memories are at the surface, others seem deeply buried or forgotten. Personal reflections fill moments that lurk and fight for attention like clouds chasing the sun to cast shadows on my sunny days. Some experiences from those early years are still waiting for expression and reconciliation. These ice caps remain visible at the surface, waiting for a triggering event. Forgiving can bring to light invisible emotions felt but not seen.

Disparities at home only partially carried over or materialized during grade school. Schoolteachers didn't need to discipline me excessively for being talkative or bullying classmates. Nevertheless, I do recall a few unforgettable and emotional times when things at home brought the full wrath of Mama.

A memory from age eight is as striking as if it happened yesterday. The memory centers on the kitchen in the backyard where we lived. Images of faded wooden mini-sized blinds with an inside hook fastened to an eyelet on the center window beam are vivid. One blind covered each of the two unscreened kitchen openings. Once these hinged covers swung open, anything with wings in flight could follow aromas rising from a tasty meal cooking on the wood-burning kitchen stove. They could fly right through the open window without a barrier because it didn't have a screen. Remembering this space from childhood makes me feel like that naïve, vulnerable eight-year-old girl again.

I can tell you how dark it gets in that kitchen after the sunsets, and daylight gives way to nightfall because it was my assigned short-term prison, so to speak.

The darkness was so thick and frightening. It seemed as if I needed a knife to cut it, especially when you are a frightened child awaiting the pending night darkness. Darkness that felt like a weight pressed heavily on my shoulders and chest. It didn't let me cry out for help. I could not even see my hands when I held them up to my face.

They shut the windows and locked the main door, making it hot. You felt the heat as if you were being cooked to become the next meal. This level of detail is vivid because the kitchen is where Mama locked me for an entire overnight "time-out" after I made another one of those child-like decisions in early spring.

The memory that brought this dreadful reaction from my Mama was an incident between us. It was laundry day. She set our wash workstation up on the porch of the backyard kitchen. Years later, I struggle to recall exactly why I'm in the wash area. Mama added hot water to this wringer washer; cold water ran through a hose to the washer from an outside faucet.

"Why on earth was a double-edged razor blade lying around the wash area?" I didn't know or care about why it was there. Without a doubt, I saw it there and picked it up." Now, to make this more straightforward, Mama saw it too. Yes, she even saw me pick up the blade. This prompted her to say,

"Girl, don't you cut my new water hose."

Unfortunately, curiosity overpowered this eight-year-olds "will to obey." I tried the razor blade out, and it surprised me. It worked! I only cut a tiny slit in the hose. When asked why, I do not know why. It was to test the blade's sharpness and its ability to make a hole through the hose. Or maybe it would make a tiny slit that nobody would notice. Yes, thoughts of a child without a concept or context for the result or even the leaking. There is no context about water flow and pressure through a restricted cylinder.

Correct! Of course, Mama learned about the extra pathway for water as it flowed through the hose when she used cold water again.

Punishment included a corporal Mississippi spanking and spending the overnight hours in isolation. Being locked in the kitchen and left alone throughout the night in this outside building was a frightening and traumatic experience. Was the main door locked? It didn't even cross my mind to check and see.

I was old enough to know better and understand Mama's expectations based on her direct orders. Only God knows what was happening in my head during those times. Looking back, I wonder why my mom didn't take the razor blade from me right away.

Whatever happened to me before age nine affected my social and emotional growth in high school and adulthood. My siblings and I didn't get clinical counseling, chances to mend our relationships or spiritual healing. Back then, I did not know anyone, children, or adults, who went for counseling.

Speaking as an adult forgiveness is a primary ground zero action between Mama and me. What dangling threads leading to forgiveness as a spiritual practice are available to get you started ... Scripture reading, counseling, or other forms of personal time with God?

A COMPLEX ENCOUNTER

One warm mid-summer afternoon, Mama and I visited my daddy's house. It marks my very first time meeting him. Since he completed his tour with the Army, Daddy lived in the

> "In your anger, do not sin; when you are on your beds, search your hearts be silent."
> **—Psalm 4:4 (NIV)**

white house next to the railroad tracks with his parents, Tassey and Toby, and his sister Collie. Their home was on Sixth Avenue. We walked about seven blocks south on the same street where Mama, my siblings, my stepfather, and I lived. As we entered the front door of Grandma Tassey's one-story single-family home, the delicious spicy smell of cinnamon and nutmeg greeted our nostrils.

"Someone's baking sweet potato pies", Mama said with a cheeriness in her voice to announce our arrival.

I had visited Grandmama Tassey two or three other times with older cousins, but daddy wasn't home during any of those times. I remember Grandma Tassey's house feeling like the inside of a baby's rattle and getting very noisy when trains traveled along the tracks next to her home. Luckily, today Mama and I visited at a time opposite the schedule for the neighborhood train. I want to be sure both Grandma and Daddy can hear Mama share the news about me starting grade school.

"When you pullin' those sweet potato pies out the oven Grandmama Tassey? Smell like they're about ready, right?"

We wrapped her tall slender and slightly arched frame with tight hugs; sealed with a kiss on the cheek, as she lowered her head to help our reach.

"In a few minutes," Grandma Tassey replied; then immediately turning toward me and said —

"Go in there and say hello to your daddy."

With an ear-to-ear smile, the adjacent room awaited me. I skipped into the room, hopping like a bunny rabbit, and gently landing about six feet away from him.

Dad sat in a dimly lit room without windows. Perhaps natural outdoor light streaming through a window would have brightened the area. A sofa was to the right of the doorway where my bunny hop did a forced stop because of the uneven wooden floorboards. He sat in the only chair in the room. It was brown and could swivel like a barber's chair. But he sat with his face turned towards the wall in front of me. The back of his head and the back of the chair were in full view. He appeared to be wearing a long sleeve pullover shirt, dark pants, and only the back of his shoes with their thick black soles were visible to me.

"Hi Daddy!"

After a few seconds of silence, his chair slowly turned counterclockwise in response to my voice and presence. My face still in full smile mode, Daddy's seated body now faced me when the chair stopped. The poor room lighting caused a shadow to fall across his face; making his features blurry even as he leaned slightly forward and towards me. Then he sternly said,

"That's what your Mama says."

At that moment, I felt the tone of his voice rub across my face like an eraser and wipe off my smile. My mouth seemed to fall open from the heaviness of eraser crumbs. The rubbery residue didn't bounce up in response to the hard floor but rested on the uneven boards at my feet. I heard his words. As a kid aged five, I didn't understand the depth and potential implication of what he meant. His gruff, scratchy voice startled me, as it delivered a sound. A sound of words which finally found a path as they first banged against my ear lopes.

My Daddy's words triggered quivering internal jabbing feelings, like the jolt I felt when Mama gave me an unexpected slap across my face in anger. It's a nervous sensation that fills my inside with sadness.

In this Daddy moment, I felt so embarrassed. I felt invisible. So ashamed. I wished I could disappear. My heart started pounding, and I momentarily stiffened. I didn't know how to respond. Eventually, I responded in my usual low-self-esteem manner with silence and a jittery retreat. What seemed like forever, I finally conjured up enough wherewithal to exit the room. Leaving, still puzzled, and stepping over my smile that fell to the raised floorboard. He didn't chase after me or acknowledge my leaving the room in any visible way.

"Wow! This is the first time I've ever actually seen or met him. Did I say something or do something wrong?" I could finally wonder as I returned to the room where Mama and Grandmama Tassey chatted. Neither of them asked me questions about my meet-up or talk with my dad. So, I did not give it a second thought. No reason to mention the hurtful encounter to anyone. This was the only interaction I remember having with my father. Mama never shared stories about him or how they met.

When I replay this encounter with my dad, his face remains blurry. But the painful memory continues with questions for which I will never have simple answers. During my early childhood, Mama always clarified that her current husband was my siblings' father, not mine. So, I never considered calling him daddy or felt related.

Many years later, during my adulthood, I was involved in a conversation that centered on my biological father and family relations. My youngest son and Aunt Jasmine (one of my biological father's sisters) were part of a discussion that resulted in me ordering a replacement birth certificate. I was home alone when my copy arrived. I quickly opened the envelope and hurriedly scanned the document. The State completed Mama's section, but the space for my father was blank.

What?

The gravity of daddy's words from age five danced and stomped around in my head as I looked at the blank father space on my official

Mississippi birth certificate. Reliving that meeting with daddy made me sob. I had been so sure his name clearly appeared on the original copy, which I had carelessly misplaced. Therefore, the blank space for father made it horrible — more than difficult… because I claim with assurance concerning his name occupying that space on my first copy. Did he request that his name be removed from the space? Was he really my biological father?

I felt humiliated and self-conscious — all the way back to our first meeting. It was almost as if I was experiencing public nudity. Why did I feel as if I had done something wrong or dishonest to cause that stunning response during my visit with daddy years ago?

Now I must share this imperfect sketchy information with my youngest son and my biological father's sister, Aunt Jasmine.

During my teen years, I lived with a relative I presumed to be my biological father's older sister, Aunt Evette, and her family. From those times and throughout adulthood, I was accepted and cared for as a blood relative, by my father's family. Mama and other adults in my life always said the gentleman I met once at Grandmamma Tassey's home as a young child, was my biological father. He died when I was in my forties. We never talked again or ever saw each other again after our encounter when I was five years old.

My Aunt Evette became terribly ill during my adult years. In those final days before transitioning to her new life, Auntie clearly said during one of my last visits with her — "You need to go be with your people." What exactly did she mean? Was she suggesting that I should be more deliberate about connecting with my estranged siblings? My maternal grandmother was already dead at this point in our journey. Or was she telling me I really wasn't an official member of her family?

We never fully understand the complexities of another's behavior. I choose to bypass the emotional road most traveled and the weight of the baggage it requires. Because of God's universal unconditional love, I extend God's grace to the memory of my father. I continue seeking ways to put this and other family heritage questions to rest.

Passages from God's word and family research by others help me find comfort.

Forgiveness:

In these moments of introspection, Scripture calls us to be deliberate about focusing our attention on God. God's word does not demand that we deny the hurt, or the pain caused by a wrong ... but hurtful pain can become a tool to help us unearth and then pull the grace of God forward and allow it to equip us to extend and accept God's grace. God extends LOVE as an invitation and lifts it beyond the pain we so easily seek to repeatedly pickup and carry. What is God's LOVE calling you to let go, again?

SHAME FUELED RESILIENCE

Great is the Lord, and greatly to be praised,
and his greatness is unsearchable.
One generation shall commend your works to another,
and shall declare your mighty acts.
On the glorious splendor of your majesty,
and on your wondrous works, I will meditate.
They shall speak of the might of your awesome deeds,
and I will declare your greatness.
They shall pour forth the fame of your abundant
goodness and shall sing aloud of your righteousness.
– Psalm 145:3-7 (ESV)

Capturing images from our early childhood for some of us is like seeing those years in a rearview mirror. At least, I continually push those acts of shame aside to allow resiliency to rise to the surface. It's not beneficial for us to bounce back in the same manner a careful definition of resiliency might imply. We seek ways for those pitfalls galvanized by humiliation

"What do we need to know and understand in order to build resilience to shame? How do we connect with our authentic selves and build meaningful connections with others?"
– Brene Brown, Ph.D., LMSW

and embarrassment to spring us forward. Forward into another orbit with frills associated with living life as we've never experienced it.

Though we don't have a written note or remember every detail, we have enough tidbits about the impact of our past on our present to do an analysis. The type of review which could help us examine the origin of how we learn not to accept and love ourselves. It is plausible that an early exposure to negative mindsets led me to align my identity with the opinion of naysayers. Learning to set proper boundaries is an essential lifelong thriving skill.

My siblings and I shared the same maternal grandmother who passed away over twenty years ago. Drawing from the grandparent roles shared by other families, our maternal grandmother didn't give us a lot of affection and encouragement. Her medium brown skin complexion and slightly overweight five three frame moved around energetically, or as some might say, she had pep in her step. Her savvy mannerisms

Influencer Generation
by Meka Ruse
highlighting Psalm 145:3-7

God placed grandparents
in family trees.
They nurture and cultivate
moral character.
And kindle civic mindedness.
Sprinkled like young flowers,
Grands stretch their tender
arms toward heaven's light,
where curiosity gives shapes of delight!
You are wonderfully and
beautifully made.
A grandparent's chirps
make all things right!
Oh, how bright our smiles as,
Gramme's words fall from trusted lips,
one generation to the ears
and heart of another!
When grandparents secretly
vex their words.
Our tomorrows lack
sweetness and wax cold.
Oh, let there be Gramme charms!
In the realities of all our
generational ears!

7

netted her: a small profitable café, a three-bedroom home with a living room, kitchen, and indoor plumbing (a tremendous deal in the 1950s for southern Blacks, and other property she rented to an auto shop business; all while living at the corner of Nineteenth and Twenty Street in a small town near Starkville, Mississippi.

Personal one-on-one interactions with Nana hold a neutral rather than positive, negative or inspirational space in my childhood memory. Her soft-throaty second soprano speaking voice and folded arm greeting stance during interactions kept me puzzled about how to approach her. I'm just not sure whether she liked me as a person. Heated arguments between her and Mama, and later between Nana and her older sister, Auntie Carrie Lou, have immediate recall. I didn't understand the adult language that peppered their interactions, but the tone of their voices and hand gestures made me a weary soul. One such interaction between Nana and Auntie Carrie Lou ended with – "A bird can fly high, but sooner or later it will need to come low to get a drink of water," Auntie Carrie Lou said to her sister, which was my Nana.

As Nana's first set of grandchildren, my siblings and I bore the brunt of our family's disputes and early dysfunction. Trying to reconcile how this happened; reaching for grandmotherly wisdom passed on to me is not helpful. My cultural grooming tool bag doesn't have a zipper compartment with this kind of wisdom. I find no tablets of seasoned generational wisdom deposited in my repertoire.

Forgiveness: A Philosophical Exploration
by Charles L. Griswold

"Forgiveness is a virtue important in an outlook that underlines our irremediable human imperfection. It responds to an aspect of imperfection (wrongdoing, evil) and expresses our imperfection. Under ideal conditions for forgiveness, there could be commitment without yielding ideal results. There might be multiple conditions under which the offender does not ask for forgiveness, such as deceased offenders face recapturing one's peace and respect by forgiving."

Why? Well, my primary memory of our maternal grandmother is not about pulling grandkids close, but it is about someone who found it fulfilling to push us, her first set of grandchildren, away. She spearheaded early adult decisions that set barriers to my siblings and I benefiting from the nurturing arms of my Mama's core family, especially her well-educated siblings. Adults in my personal orbit couldn't foresee the future impact of their decisions. And research about the long arm of family trauma wasn't available. The damage reaches into the hollow path of our disjointed childhood journey day after day after day; then it moved into years of painful family history.

My reality hadn't readily provided wisdom inspired by lived experiences at this point. Yet, my lived experiences have washed me ashore on the wings of God's merciful love. There is tucked away here a required set of healthy practices. These actions bring me face to face with Jesus' model of "The F-Word" for all believers ...FORGIVENESS! It expanded a commitment to dig deeper to understand forgiveness. It calls me to sit at the feet of Jesus for nurturing. I will grapple with scars etched by shame to receive the special set of grandmotherly tools needed. God will surely invigorate what I have tried to set at a distance because now I too, must take up the mantle of being "a grandmother."

Great is the LORD and most worthy of praise; his greatness no one can fathom.

One generation commends your works to another;
they tell of your mighty acts.

> **What constitutes a family secret? When might a hidden truth need to be exposed?**

They speak of the glorious splendor of your majesty—
and I will meditate on your wonderful works.[a]
They tell of the power of your awesome works—
and I will proclaim your great deeds.
They celebrate your abundant goodness
and joyfully sing of your righteousness.

Psalm 145:3–7 (NIV)

ACTS OF GIVING
ONE'S VOICE AWAY

Happy are those whose transgression is forgiven, whose
sin is covered. Happy are those to whom the Lord imputes
no iniquity, and in whose spirit, there is no deceit.
– Psalm 32:1-2 (NRSV).

While colleagues developed false narratives about my background, my attempts at correcting them required more energy and unveiling than I wanted to invest in our relationships. I've been guilty of staying awkwardly vague and intentionally distant when those situations arise. Especially when I believed the alternative would not generate enough positive energy to keep me engaged. Why have I thought it okay to let wrong impressions

> **Never give your voice away!**
>
> When forgiveness becomes a delayed reaction, it's a debt that will continue collecting fees. For some of us, this could turn into a lifetime without resolve for what we call "outstanding issues." No one is exempt. Especially when you are the vessel promoting the Gospel of Christ Jesus and within the context of the price he's already paid, forgiveness must always be an intentional action between God, others, and yourself.

and misinformation float in the atmosphere? Why do we often think our story isn't worth telling?

I took notice of how I lived out this quote from Positive Enthusiasm: "You cannot heal your wounds if you are busy hiding them!" Here's where I had to commit to own my destructive actions…

Here's a dinner chat at a Kiwanis event when I was serving my second year as Treasurer of the Southeastern Ohio group…" Hi, Mark. Is it okay if I take this open seat next to you? Are you expecting family?"

"Oh, sure Meka. It's okay. I'm not expecting anyone."

"How long have you and your family operated your warehouse company?"

"Over fifty years. My father started the business and passed it on to me and my brother. It's been a lot of work but rewarding for keeping a roof over our head and food on the table", Mark said with a smile.

"You born and raised here in this area?"

"Yes, my family lived on the westside during my childhood. We had a typical upbringing … much like yours."

Those words he used, "typical much like yours," gave me a brain freeze. Thus, I altered my impromptu conversational gesture to guard my pierced feelings. We continued to chat, but I lacked the fortitude to fully engage and correct his error in assumption about my childhood.

A lack of action resonates with profiles of people who develop and coddle pangs of a miserable existence, not realizing it's a home without protective walls. Are you investing in a home with God's protective walls?

Another example that supported my resolve to maintain a distance between me and others happened during my tenure as pastor. I felt relaxed enough to chime in on sharing with our United Methodist District Superintendent, clergy and laity. They were sharing tidbits about their childhood experiences of being spanked by their parents. I was feeling very comfortable in my skin, or so I thought anyway. I talked about being spanked by Mama with plaited peach tree switches. "When the switches broke, Mama didn't miss a stroke," I said. I continued to be beaten until my mother grabbed the closest impromptu weapon, a metal lid lifter used for wood stoves. Two whacks to my face with that object drew blood and frightened her enough to hold up on the licks and resort to her standard yelling."

"Oh, please stop talking," our District Superintendent said.

"Why?", I asked. No further response or input from him. *Wow, did I say something wrong? I thought to myself. Should I continue trying to share my truth?*

One more type of "keep your upbringing to yourself" came when I used one of my childhood experiences during a youth session at a church where I pastored. Ninety-nine percent of children taking part in ministry at our church were members of struggling households. But youth responded to my personal example with, "Oh! That is so so sad." What I thought would inspire clearly had the opposite effect. From that point forward, I vowed to cease from attempts to share from the deep treasures of my life. Even when others seemed to carve an opening for sharing, I resisted. I wanted no one's piety. By now, it had become obvious that my childhood "normal" didn't have a thread of commonality among other households or adults in my circle. My sense of having an unusual background made me question my self-worth, and a simmering distaste for the status quo festered.

Where has shame taken you? Where did you seek encouragement as a child? Who have you used the power of shame to control?

Forgiveness: Rest in God's Loving Care.

Grandmama Sally Ann, may you rest in peace as the spirit of forgiveness showers the brokenness of our family with God's unending love, grace, and mercy. I daily lay before God's throne of grace, seeking to release the toxins from this to be forever unresolved and unanswerable family decision.

HOPEFUL DAYS

"People have heard my groaning, but there is no one to
comfort me. All my enemies have heard of my distress;
they rejoice at what you have done. May you bring the day
you have announced so they may become like me."
—Lamentations 1:21 (NIV)

Yes, I obviously had earlier childhood years. There aren't
family pictures, letters, or journals to assist with reliving
those days and times. Perusing national events provided a
timestamp, and a context helped me revisit those years.

On a Monday morning in September in the mid 1950's, like
many other homes, my family was up early to get me ready for
school. The Baby Boom caused a need for 167,000 schools across the
United States to house 29 million kids. They built Union Academy
in 1877 specifically for African American K-8 grade students to
be taught by African American teachers. They converted it to an
elementary school in 1954.

In our home, the sun's colorful reflection splattered against the
walls like paint from a spinning dispenser. Light passed through
the front window from a clear blue sky and magnified the cheerful
mood already set in motion for this special morning. My mama and
stepfather rented our one-room living space in a home owned by
Miss Latham and her father. Our two families shared this single-
story house with four large rooms. It had two rooms on each side of

a long, well-lit hallway with an unobstructed view from the front door to the backyard.

The first large room to the left made me feel safe each time I walked across its threshold. My six-member core family and I played, slept, ate, and bathed in this cozy space. Without the aid of the dancing sunlight, the walls were dull off-white, nearing a light gray color, but the morning sun is on special duty today. Mama had the furniture arranged with her full-sized bed in a corner next to the window facing the front porch. Another window on the right wall, a little lower, allowed you to gaze inside while standing outside in the yard with the aid of a ladder or on your friend's shoulder. We positioned Mama's four-drawer dresser here to create space in the center of the room for the roll-away bed we used every night. On this first day of school, the Mississippi cloudless sky was making our family living space glow with happiness and excitement!

Everyone in the room is relishing the joyous spirit of the moment and the result of my pre-school test. I'm starting first grade at Union Academy Elementary School. And get this, I am still only five years old. Okay, in the larger scheme of things, my sixth birthday is coming in October. The State Department of Education set the birthday cut-off date. My academic level helped too.

Mama is so pleased about me clearing enrollment to become a five-year-old first grader. A few days ago, I overheard her say to Miss Latham—"Meka's elementary school, Union Academy, has two-levels for new students, high first and first grade. Based on my understanding," she continued, "Meka tests high enough academically to be in the regular first grade class with those six-year-old students."

In a few hours, I will officially begin my first day of school, making her proud! My ear-to-ear trademark smile shows off all my pearly whites! I'm quickly reciting my polite manners skills, which Mama says always start with turning on my listening ears ... *I feel so happy inside when Mama smiles back at me. My siblings and Mama are turning my heart into a cheerful smiley face! The way everyone lets me be first in line for important things like washing my face, brushing my teeth, and getting breakfast makes me feel special. HOORAY!!! Everyone is exploding with excitement because I'm the first child among us to start school!*

They added the final touches for my school debut: the outfit, lunch and school supplies made it a finished task. David and Mandy are scurrying around, making sure sharpened pencils, paper, and a composition tablet are in the designated book satchel. It was time to sit attentively on the floor in front of Mama's chair between her legs to have my hair combed and braided after breakfast. She parted it in three sections, then made one large braid in the top that hung down in my face below my eyebrows and one on each side, landing above each ear.

Now it was time to put on that brand new dark brown scoop front jumper and a white blouse with a puffy ruffle down the front covering the row of white buttons. A new pair of black and white saddle oxfords rounded out the school outfit. Mama did all the school shopping at a dime store called McClelland's. Now, we are ready to take on this new adventure as one big, happy family.

"Meka, iron this ribbon so you can wear a bow in your hair," Mama said as she laid a multi-colored striped wrinkled ribbon on the ironing board.

Moving the warm iron over the wrinkles made them disappear. But then the ribbon started getting wrinkly again. Now, I didn't know why it did that. It frightened me watching this happen. Mama looked over, checking the progress, and could see the ribbon reacting to the heat.

Mama yelled! "Stop ironing it!" She walked towards me and followed up with a pounding hand slap on the back of my head. Come on, what're you doing?"

"Can't you do anything right?" This is how I learned the beautifully colored hair ribbon was burning.

I started crying in response to the slap and yelling.

"Stop crying!" Mama hollered.

The pain from the slap on my head hurt. But it was dull compared to the hurt I felt in my heart every time Mama yelled at me for disappointing her.

Besides yelling and slapping our face, Mama also spanked us with switches or belts, like most parents in my neighborhood. Painful spankings with belts, switches or the back of your parent's hands were among the methods used for child-rearing in my household. But my greatest scars came from being yelled at by adults in charge of my wellbeing. Or when they used humiliating labels and would tell me to be quiet as I cried in response to the pain in my heart.

As time moved forward, whether I was seeking help with homework or asking to go outside to play, I learned that asking follow-up questions was a sure way to receive punishment from an adult care giver managing my life. Sometimes Mama's help with Math homework was confusing when she explained the steps for doing subtraction. What did "take away" mean, anyway? When we were looking at a set on numbers in columns, it didn't make sense to me at the time? Questions would raise her ire.

Forgiveness

Taking Out Your Emotional Trash (2010) by Georgia Shaffer

We seek quick solutions, yet this cannot acknowledge the healing needed for our soul's wounds. We must commit to doing the work necessary to bring about healing. In life, the trauma caused by abusive relationships, even from childhood, that build-up pressure within us needs to be released slowly.

As I think about the time we had with you, Mama, I am determined to invest more energy into learning how to keep extending forgiveness to both you and me and others. It's a slow intentional process. The process requires taking a personal smile each time my life seems to turn upside down and shaken like a carbonated beverage. Learning to give it time to settle slowly before reengaging the grind helps us refresh.

The Forgiveness Project is helping me learn more about myself and it has helped me recognize Mama's pain.

ABOUT MAMA

Considering what we've learned over the years, Mama's behaviors may have been signs or calls for help. She didn't have many resources and needed her family's help. Yes, her actions were in plain sight

> The end of a matter is better than its beginning, and patience is better than pride. Do not be quickly provoked in your spirit, for anger resides in the lap of fools. **Ecclesiastes 7:8–9 (NIV)**

to every adult around her, but her genuine pain remained invisible to everyone in her life. Now, as an adult, I am looking back at her own historic journey superimposed on those years with Mama.

Some things hang between our decades by a common thread of self-worth. The method of reflecting makes some things about those times clearer. A schema for looking back and then forward can give one whiplash. But it is the use of this method that makes connecting with my past an acceptable process. I believe Mama's expressions of love were overshadowed by her greatest fears. At the top of her list of importance was providing us with a balanced diet, shelter, and clothing. So, living with the reality of coming up short on basic resources, followed by Mama's own need for love and respect, were heavy emotional weights for her.

Through my process of trial and error to better understand, Mama seemed to have learned how to provide a healthy lifestyle for her children. This included daily meals, a solid education, safety from negativity, and the warmth of family. But Mama operated from a list of Plan Bs, which made it confusing for little ones to adhere to or understand.

More than a few times, we implemented Plan B when she didn't have food at home or money in her purse for school lunch. My role-play in one of mama's alternative plans meant following instructions, asking no questions. Especially those times when she directed me to include a stop at a house on Fifteenth Street on my walk to school. On Fifteenth Street, I became acquainted with this exceptionally large antebellum style house. Its main entrance led me into a short hall. There were stairs immediately to my right. They seemed to disappear into the darkness as they stretched to the upper floors. They had replaced the windowpanes in the hallway door with tan plywood, making the entryway void of natural bright morning light. I didn't feel as safe here as I did in the hallway at our home. I hurriedly walked down this short foyer to the last room on the left and knocked on the door as instructed by Mama.

"When the gentleman responds to your knocking, say to him, I am Linda's daughter and I need lunch money for school."

Walks to school regularly included stops at the big house on Fifteenth Street during my second and third-grade school years. I never officially saw or even met the gentlemen. He simply remained the man behind the door to me because he would always keep his faced hidden; his door ajar; an opening just wide enough for his light-brown adult-sized chubby hand with short fingers and manicured nails, to reach my teeny kid-size hand to receive the two dimes and a nickel I needed for school lunch. Mama never introduced us or explained who he was; even when I asked her. But, one day after placing twenty-five cents for lunch in my hand, in a mid-range male voice, he said,

"Tell your Mama she should stop sending you by here to ask for money."

I gladly relayed his message directly to Mama. That ended my stops at the house on Fifteenth Street.

Another time, I remember Mama showing anxiousness about

resources was during her chitchat with neighbors. I overheard her in conversation with neighbors discussing the difficulty and accompanying stress; she felt about meeting the basic needs of her family. Maybe she thought those were private adult conversations. Although I heard them. One day she explained to the neighbor that her paycheck from the laundry was not enough money to cover rent and buy food. These overheard conversations are where I learned my stepfather was an alcoholic. His disease interfered with his ability to hold steady employment.

Mama had a sense of humor, too. The Military Street Laundry, where she worked, had a weekly pay system. They distributed payroll in cash rather than paper checks. Employers placed cash payments in small manila envelopes. In one of her neighborly chitchats, Mama told a story about walking home from work.

"I almost dropped my envelope in the sewer grate as I walked down the sidewalk on Fifteenth Street," she shared in her southern paced alto voice: "They would arrest me for tearing up the street if my money had fallen in that sewer drain. I would make such a fuss; folks would think I had lost my mind."

"Boy, that would look pretty funny seeing Mama's tall lanky brown skin body on her knees tearing up the street with her bare hands trying to retrieve her money," I wanted to laugh out loud but couldn't because, remember, I'm invisible listening to this adult conversation. Playing in the front yard near Mama's feet as she talked to our neighbor was a place to keep track of family affairs.

In another look back at Mama's signs of stressful toil, was she hankered for wholesome relationships with her own siblings and her mother, too. Mama and Nana often had a shouting style of talking to each other, which ended up in arguments. I never knew what caused their screaming and hostile resentment. But I remember my Mama getting so upset one day, she told all of us to call our Nana by her given first name, "Miss Sally Ann" rather than Nana. She retracted this mandate after a few weeks. At least we didn't have to call our grandmother by her first name for those remaining years of Mama's life. Although, I'm sad to report that the discord never completely found harmony during my early years. This darkness still follows us.

On a visit home one summer during my adult years, Aunt Evette, a paternal auntie, pulled me aside for a one-on-one chat about my mother's family history. I was clueless about the potential content since no one briefed me beforehand. Turns out, she wanted to talk about Mama's side of the family. Specifically, about the toxic relationship between my Mama and her mother (Nana).

> I was in my early forties and perhaps *I thought to myself, Aunt Evette has some information about estate matters associated with my mother and her siblings that's led to internal family friction.*

She opened with, "Your Mama was Miss Sally Ann's first-born child. Basically, your grandmother was an unwed mother. Miss Sally Ann married Mr. Williams when your mother was somewhere between ten and thirteen. Linda was not a welcome member of Miss Sally Ann's new family. So, she gave Linda away to some people in Alabama. Maybe it was a legal adoption, I don't really know. But Linda used their last name, Curtis, which was the same as the Alabama family. She used Curtis as her official last name until she married Nathaniel."

I felt anxious; this was awkward because my maternal grandmother, Nana, was still alive at this time and she had offered none of this information about Mama's early childhood. We sat in my Aunt Evette's living room in the quiet of this Mississippi summer afternoon while I regained my composure. Then she continued …

"Linda ran away after living there in Alabama for about three years and found her way back home to Mississippi. She came back to the city where she had family, but Linda hadn't made plans for a place to live. Maybe she didn't even know whom to reach out to and ask for help once she was back. Life in Alabama must have been unpleasant. Seems like Linda would rather linger at the local

Trailways bus station in her Mississippi hometown than stay with her abusive foster parents in Alabama."

"What?" I said in a raised voice filled with disbelief. Without responding to my question, my aunt continued.

"Linda eventually accepted an invitation from a stranger for a place to sleep overnight. That unidentified stranger contacted Miss Sally Ann's older sister, Carrie Lou. It was Carrie Lou and her husband who let Linda live with them for two years. Well, at least until she was on the path to becoming a single mother herself. When she was expecting you, they sent Linda away to live in Yazoo, Mississippi. This is where you were born in a local hospital. One of your delivery nurses named you Meka."

At this point in my listening session, the emptiness and pain I was feeling made my face ache as Aunt Evette and I sat there with our seats facing each other, but not within arm's reach. There was no hugging or even warm words offered to comfort each other. The afternoon shadow made it difficult for us to see each other's facial expressions. But the tension in the air was noteworthy as I cradled my aching face in my hands. This limited disclosure was causing a deep ache. In a loud trembling voice …

"I am shocked; surprised beyond belief about what I'm hearing you say. These details about Mama's early years are so sad." Why didn't you tell me sooner?"

"Well, I really thought you had already heard about this," she expounded in a breathed answer.

This exposing of family drama was heart breaking; tore it into a thousand pieces. My eyes welded with tears as I kept my head in my hands. During the silence I pondered and wondered, *why didn't Nana or any Mama's family members think it important to share these details with me? This revelation brought context to Mama's adulthood and challenging early childhood.*

My head was over hyped from Mama's family members, especially Nana and Mama's siblings, being quick to degrade Mama's role as a parent. They seemed to work overtime to create and sustain a gap between Mama's offspring and our maternal cousins. Mama seemed to have an acceptable relationship with Aunt Carrie Lou. Yet, it was Aunt Carrie Lou who often told me, while I lived with her from age nine to twelve:

"I'm doing more for you than your Mama ever did!"

My emotional reaction to this new information brought the session to an abrupt silence and a full stop. I never reached a place where I felt mentally healthy enough to extend a prompt to my Aunt Evette to complete this important story during her lifetime. I have never heard the remaining specifics to fill in the breaks in the scenario about Mama's early years. Mandy was unsuccessful in her attempts to locate Mama's Alabama family. Information about Mama's separation from her birth family is scarce. We have no family pictures of Mama from any period during her twenty-eight years on this earth.

Same as many families we read about, our older maternal family members kept tons of secrets about family lineage; details like extended family connections and their parents before moving to Mississippi. Who were those foster parents? Not sure whether this spotty keeping of historical records is on par with most African American southern families. However, without a doubt, Mama had a painful childhood, was a frustrated parent, and an abused wife. Other potential holders of early family tree information are deceased or dealing with memory loss because of old age.

My mother's music taste sheds light on her love for us and fears about her basic quality of life. Mama would recline on the bed in our one-room living space and close her eyes when she listened to music that she liked. Her favorite listening moments worked best for her when the kids were all outside playing. She repeatedly played a song by the Platters – "Oh Yes, I'm a Great Pretender." She would turn the volume up on that old RCA vintage record player so that all within the vicinity of our house could hear it. That old record player would spin this vinyl 78 and the music filled the air with …

Oh-oh, yes, I'm the great pretender
Pretending that I'm doing well
My need is such I pretend too much
I'm lonely but no one can tell
Oh-oh, yes, I'm the great pretender
Adrift in a world of my own
I've played the game but to my real shame
You've left me to grieve all alone
Too real is this feeling of make-believe
Too real when I feel what my heart can't conceal
Yes, I'm the great pretender
Just laughin' and gay like a clown
I seem to be what I'm not, you see
I'm wearing my heart like a crown
Pretending that you're still around

We will never know all there is to know, but I can surmise through this look back that Linda's life was terribly complex. Mama's quality of life and her known frustrations spilled over into her survival tactics and expressions of care for us.

In retrospect, despite Mama's complex life, she worked five days a week at a dry cleaner on Military Street. Several neighbors have helped us confirm that Mama was an extremely dedicated employee and parent. She kept our one rented room immaculate. Four of us slept in a roll-away bed. Each morning, Mama expected us to make the bed and then fasten the head and foot together using the metal flap on top before storing it in the right corner of the room. All before washing our face.

She often thought about moving to Birmingham, Alabama, for a fresh start for herself and her children. I did not understand why life in a neighboring city and state would be better for us. We never experienced her hopeful thoughts about relocating as an intact family during her lifetime. I can't be sure why, but even at my young age, I felt my stepfather wouldn't be part of our relocation.

We don't have pictures of Mama. For this reason and those

unspoken, unshared ones too, I enter the following graphic as part of this publication in honor of my Mama.

Anger: Handling a Powerful Emotion in a Healthy Way by Gary Chapman ...

Chapman's work supports the notion that the source of much of our anger falls under the category of being distorted. Distorted anger... the perceived injustice might be feelings nestled in our own presumptions and expectations of others. Thus, we feel wronged when we don't close the gate or try to deny entry in our own private space. Over time, distorted anger can cause us to react as though this is a sinful or immoral act, but the hope is that we learn to take a moment to gather more facts about our power to manage these intrusions before they turn into rage.

Forgiveness

Passive aggressive behavior is borne out of implosion anger. Anger is a visitor, never a long-term resident in one's heart. We are visited by this firm sense of justified anger when we neglect setting appropriate boundaries. In too many cases, we let the family into this space and expect them to enter with a nurturing spirit. That doesn't happen! Dr. Gary Chapman sets a perspective to help unravel anger as an emotion we learn to move beyond and move closer to embracing forgiveness.

A TURN OF EVENTS

Let my teaching fall like rain and my words descend like
dew, like showers on new grass, like abundant rain on
tender plants. I will proclaim the name of the Lord.
–Deuteronomy 32:2-3 (NIV).

Without explanation or opportunity for questions, we
had an unexpected event that would change our lives.
It started on the morning of an overcast day when Miss
Latham nervously said— "You kids go sit on the porch" … while
gently touching my shoulder for me to lead my sisters and brothers
in single file, we walked from her bedroom, down the long hall.
We passed our home base for years; a fun, familiar space for us. She
walked slightly ahead of me down the hall as we left her bedroom,
heading for the front porch. *It was unusual for us to wake up in Miss
Latham's bedroom. Other adults were scurrying around the hall, in and out
of our large, all-purpose room. But none of them, except Miss Latham, seem
to notice us. No one made eye contact with us or shared why we spent the
night in Miss Latham's bedroom. What made our rented space off limits this
morning? Where was Mama?*

*So, I'm following Miss Latham, but subconsciously feeling unsettled, I
am rehearsing the rules Mama taught us about honoring which rooms were
off-limits in the house. But why were we waking up in bed in one of those
off-limit rooms? Did Mama give Miss Latham permission to take us to her
bedroom while we were barely awake last night? Miss Earnestine, lives around*

the corner on 20th Street. Why was she visiting so early? Had she stayed overnight with Miss Latham, too? This was a very confusing morning for my siblings and me. We walked out to the front porch as instructed. All five of us squeezed our teeny bodies into the bench-shaped suspended swing.

I contorted my nine-year-old body like a pretzel for one foot to reach the floor and slowly pumped the back-and-forth motion of the swing. Anyone walking along the gravel street could see us seated there and read the confusion stamped on our faces. They could see the gentle movement of the swing intended to comfort my sisters and brothers seated with me.

"Why can't we go inside?" my younger sister Candy asked.

"It's cold out here," Mandy added.

"I'm cold and hungry, too. Stop whining."

Hours seem to have passed, but still none of those adults had been forthcoming with information about why we needed to stay outside on the front porch. And no one has offered us food for breakfast! *Where is Mama? I asked in my head.*

My siblings started making their wishes known again ...

"I want to go inside, too," Rufus said.

"We can't, I already TOLD YOU!" I whispered emotionally in a low stern voice. Miss Latham told us to come out here and wait in the swing."

"It's cold out here. Why can't we go inside?" Several of them said in unison.

My mind kept recycling what I thought I knew - each family had their own private space within the house. But late last night, Miss Latham, my stepfather, and Miss Earnestine must have interrupted the sleep of the sleep of all five of us. I remember going to sleep in our roller-away bed last night. But we finished the night in Miss Latham's personal bed. I barely remember taking the few steps from my bed to Miss Latham's bed during the night because I never fully awakened from my sleep. Just gingerly aroused enough to be led by the hand without needing to follow commands. A trademark during my early years. For instance, I remember literally falling out of bed onto a wood floor during the night and never waking until the next day. At which time, I found myself under the bed. I was still stunned. This was so odd. Where was Mama? This had never happened before. I didn't see my stepdad this morning.

But today's circumstances were taking an unfortunate turn for me and our entire family. This day began awkwardly, with a considerable level of uncertainty and confusion among the adults. The morning didn't clear up; just seemed to grow murky and deeply dark. The mood of my personal morning matched the mood of the overcast April sky. I remember noticing and feeling the gloom of the moment while we impatiently waited in a swing, which we seldom used, on a familiar porch that we loved to play on.

The weather and location really were unusual to us, but being outside in the swing early in the morning rather than inside with Mama having breakfast was unfamiliar territory. Why the in the world couldn't we go inside? Did we do something wrong?

I don't know how long we sat in that swing, but it seemed like an eternity to my restless siblings and me. Eventually, our Nana appeared outside the gate that led to our front yard.

"Good morning."

"Good morning, Nana," we all responded in unison.

"You kids come on and get in my car. Don't worry about bringing anything with you right now. "You all just come on right now and go with me." We finally left the swing, stepped off the front porch to climb into Nana's two-tone green four-door Buick. We took a four-block drive to Nana's house.

I would later overhear conversations between my Nana and other adults and learn our mother had died during the previous night. Mama had died giving birth to twins in our all-purpose room. She gave birth to a healthy baby girl (Sally). A baby boy was stillborn.

"Mama is dead. What does all this mean for us?" As I pretended not to hear the adult conversation in the next room, I pondered to myself. I didn't dare openly ask my grandmother questions about it. Screaming adults responding to my questions kept me muted, while my brain raged with anxiety. Especially when it's clear that I was not being spoken to. I hated being yelled at.

The time never came when my siblings and I were officially called together to hear about Mam's death; a grieving session or any type of emotional support where we could ask questions; nor a time to be briefed on pending decisions later made on our behalf. Our reality now was all six of us would live together with our maternal grandmother. In the coming days, I overheard other conversations to the contrary between Nana and other adults.

"I can't keep Linda's kids. I can't take care of all these kids," we overheard Nana saying with a chuckle in many adult conversations. *This chuckle was the way she affixed her declarative statements, I later learned.* Her words still ring in my ears and raise unanswered questions.

During those times, Mandy and Rufus would repeatedly ask me with exactness, "When are we going home?" And, literally saying, "I want to go home."

It felt like a stinging hurt in my heart each time they asked because of the adult conversations that were overheard. Repeatedly telling them we were not going back to our shared living space on Sixth Avenue just didn't register with them. My brothers and sisters were very important to me. It was difficult to remember whether I did a good job comforting them while I, too, was living deep in their same shared pain.

Nana's home had three bedrooms, a kitchen, and a living room. There wasn't a hallway between rooms. A shared wall and one doorway separated these living spaces at grandma's house. There were two doorways that led to the kitchen and living room. Her home had an indoor toilet, too. Whereas we sensed the environment at Nana's home as appealing to the eye because it was a house of many rooms; more spread-out than any place we had ever called home; yet it did not provide the welcome and caring spirit similar to what we associated with the meaning of home with Mama.

I did not have an adult level understanding of what the death of a custodial parent would mean. It was a circumstance destined for us; with me being the oldest at age nine.

This life experience alongside my younger siblings quickly grew beyond our control and understanding. We lived this experience from the underside of life's definition of family and the lack of nurturing childhood support systems. It still makes me tear up and some days, openly sob. Some use the beautiful design on the topside of a quilt to explain life. Currently, we were clearly living and seeing life from the underside of a handcrafted quilt. Lots of knots, leading to no place; and gaps in connections and supports.

Requiring silence about the death of my Mama meant zero discussions with the adults in charge. The mode of operation seemed to be keep moving and be strong. Many nights I cried myself to sleep. Then feeling sad during the school day while thinking that kids were mean to me because my Mama had died. Our father/stepfather was alive, but he disappeared during this critical time of transition.

I slept on the living room sofa while living at Nana's house. This is where I dreamed about Mama shortly after her death. She was standing near a large body of water; like standing near an ocean. It looked like she was on a beach with blue water gently moving in the background. She spoke words to me; I heard her voice, but I could not understand what she was saying. She disappeared as I attempted to let her know I did not understand what she said. I remember waking up to the sound of my voice as I was talking to mama in my sleep, during a dream. This was my one and only dream about her.

Mama's funeral was some days later at a church where Nana was on staff as the pianist. Another humiliation came during preparation for Mama's funeral services. Nana nor anyone else in the family had a picture of Mama to use on the bulletin cover for her funeral services. This was another point of pain because Nana had pictures of all her other children displayed on top of the piano in her living room. But not one picture of our Mama.

As younger children, we did not understand the formality or finality of a funeral. I remember it being a sad occasion because many people were crying. After all these years, I still remember the last song sang at the funeral—"Lord, I'm Coming Home." It was the recessional song sang as Mama's casket exited the church. I remember little about the actual content of the funeral service, except sobbing and sobbing an awful lot.

Trauma is a psychological wound to a child. All wounds take time to heal. We should give children the time they need to process

MEKA RUSE, EdD

because the wound created by a trauma is much like what needs to happen when there's a broken bone.[3] Healing from wounds require time, understanding, support and protection. My siblings and I would have welcomed loving support or counseling to nurture our spiritual wellbeing through the trauma of losing our Mama. Our core adult relatives left each one of us to deal with this grief in his or her own way. Nana navigated the next important step in our lives. She spearheaded working with her inner circle and core members of the community to find homes for all six of her grandchildren. Nana's home was the very last place that we lived together as brothers and sisters. This was late spring and into early summer 1957. With our separation came personal requests for a new identity for siblings by some of the adoptive families.

Where was my stepfather during this ordeal? He did not seem to care about Nana giving his own kids away to strangers. I never remember having negative interactions with him. But wow! My siblings are his flesh and blood, too!

Flipping through memories of my early childhood 60+ years after Mama's passing, has allowed me to recall and relive the associated hurts. My memory is scratchy about the chain of events immediately following Mama's death.

Reconciliation

God called Mama to heaven when she was twenty-eight and her offspring numbered seven, all under the age of ten. We are grateful for our time with her. Since her journey here, our number is now five. May God continue walking with us; teaching us to thrive; keeping us focused on possibilities and mindfully fit to see the greater good. Amen.

---

[3] Monahon, Cynthia (1993). *Children and Trauma: A Guide for Parents and Professional.* Pg. 7-8, Jossey-Bass.

So, teach us to count our days so that we may gain a wise heart. (Psalm 90:12 NRSV) Are you still teachable?

MY CHILDHOOD:
ADULTHOOD PTSD?
MY FIRST JOB

"If you, O Lord, should mark iniquities, Lord, who
could stand? But there is forgiveness with you, so that
you may be revered." (Psalm 130:4 NRSV)

Children who experience lifestyle altering circumstances like witnessing the death of a sibling, domestic violence, a lack of food or even the lack of the rallying cheer of a caring person, miss out on identifying triggers for compassion. But deep within me, it's my nature to want to fix everything for others. I know I can't. These life events create sores that might scab over but will never heal until they receive intentional focus. Scabbed over sores pepper my soul and form barriers to influencing my inner wellbeing. Posttraumatic stress among children was not a common area of study during my formative years.

A traumatic event is a necessary precursor for developing posttraumatic stress disorder (PTSD), a psychological condition linking potentially traumatizing events. Researchers now believe symptoms increase with traumatic events, prompting feelings of guilt and shame. These emotional triggers may be associated with using coping skills centered on avoidance and disengagement.

Looking back, I wonder why I never questioned my maternal grandmother Nana's absence in my life during teen years, even though we lived within five blocks of each other. After Mama's death, Nana brought us to her home but promptly distributed us like useless items to other families. Some weren't even distant relatives. She provided oversight for placing each of us in foster care homes within three weeks of mama's death. God granted Nana a long, happy life. But we never discussed the obvious during her lifetime— why didn't she love us enough to help raise her own grandchildren? Not one of us ever lived with her. She kept a safe distance during my high school years. My other siblings continued living in our hometown after my high school graduation and departure. Perhaps their reflections might differ from mine.

I don't even remember Nana's presence or her offering well wishes at my high school graduation. Probing the why's of her decision during my visits back home after I was older never crossed my mind. But the negative chatter from those I looked to for encouragement continued tearing away at my self-worth one painful chunk of memory and event at a time well into my adult years. Were Nana's reactions towards me related to issues between her and Mama? Something wasn't settled in their grievances before Mama died. Their story line was deeply riveting whenever I heard them argue when I was younger. The distasteful folklore and narrative about me and the unpleasant framing of Mama's life contributed to my definition of what loneliness meant.

By the time I graduated high school, three of my mother's sisters were already college graduates. They were my secret inspiration. Nana had my auntie's high school and college cap and gown pictures on top of her upright piano in a nice display. Again, there wasn't one snapshot of my mother any place at Nana's house. But I thought it would be a major feat to have my cap and gown photo displayed in that place of honor. Then and even now, some relatives and I feel a painful throbbing of humiliation in our hearts whenever we're reminded that a picture of Mama was not available for her obituary. There were numerous photos available of her siblings.

Oh, how I longed to attend college. I remember my Aunt Jasmine and her husband calling me into the living room one afternoon to share in a few words, "we can't afford to send you to college." Before I could ask even one follow-up question, "We can only support you or your cousin, which you know is our son. We have arranged for Charlie to attend college in Washington State, where he will live with relatives. Plus. he's a male child and will need to provide for a family someday."

"But my grades are good enough for a scholarship at Tougaloo University, aren't they?"

"You have good grades. Part of your tuition and housing would need to be covered by a loan. It would be helpful to have some of your mom's family offer you support. But they haven't come forward offering financial support so far. Anyway, most girls marry and don't even complete their college studies. We just can't take that chance and get deep into debt," they added.

With my face contorted, I broke out into an ugly cry. Sobbing and wheezing uncontrollably, I retreated to my room. The tears flowed. They kept coming for more than an hour. I felt so disappointed. I felt so rejected and set aside. Finances or an advocate to plead my case just weren't available. The remaining days of my senior year were a blur. I had no say in shaping my future journey.

Those teen years and high school days cumulated with graduation and a move to the mid-west. This is where I would live, raise a family and work for over thirty years. Off I went on a sunny Mississippi morning, riding a Trailway Bus to find a job in a new city up north.

"They need a dishwasher at the restaurant where I work," Aunt Diane hollered upstairs to me as she was leaving one morning. "I'll tell them I'm bringing you in with me tomorrow."

"Okay," I yelled back while thinking, *I hate washing dishes.*

Having never eaten in a restaurant, I could only relate the job offer to what I knew about washing dishes at home. My assigned home chores during high school years included washing dishes after dinner. It appeared, to my teenage eyes anyway, that my Auntie Jasmine used every pot and pan in the kitchen when making those home-cooked meals. She didn't enjoy sharing the space so I could wash as she used pots, pans, and skillets. That meant piles of "stuff" to scrap and prep before dishwashing. By hand, of course. I know how to wash dishes. Well, it's fair to say that the restaurant's dish room was a bit more automated than my double sink, squeaky, faucet teenage experience at home. Didn't make me enthusiastic about the chore, though.

Weeks turned into months. But, before my restaurant dishwashing months turned into years, I landed a dishwashing job at a local hospital. We called our work area the "tray room." Our job duties included plating patients' food trays. Food choices were based on individual patient diets printed on menu cards provided by the dietitian. Members of our tray room team delivered these same meals to patients. It was a pleasure meeting and chatting briefly with patients about whatever was on their mind in those moments.

Sometimes our tray room work schedules required working a split shift: 6:30 AM—11AM; 2:30 PM—6:30 PM. I never adjusted to it. Glad we did it in rotation. My biological clock would be out of whack whenever my afternoon shift was split. I even remember showing up for work when I wasn't scheduled. Not a car owner in those days, walking to work was common practice. I was not a happy camper when I misread my schedule or took an afternoon nap and woke up, not knowing whether it was AM or PM. Perhaps this is where I gained the speed walker label. Needing to get to work on time taught me how to step with a purpose.

The hospital tray room is where I sprang forth and blossomed as someone with potential, according to those around me. My food service job eventually grew to working the cash register in the employee cafeteria. Physicians, nurses and administrators, all strangers to me, were reaching out with positive conversations. My supervisors and others expressed a willingness to assist and encouraged me to further my education. The entrenched, self-conscious emotions of guilt and shame from my childhood dimmed the brightness of their offer. So much so, I didn't know how to receive these positive gestures or how to ask for help. Their kindness just didn't match what my earlier surroundings had conditioned me to believe about myself. Now, I have these complete strangers yacking in one ear and my core childhood voices in the other. Who am I to believe?

In retrospect, I wasn't prepared to function in my real world, or anyone else's. While on the job, I was a model employee. My social network or support system had not cultivated a healthy inner self-worth voice. Sadly, I was years away from fully embracing this sphere of human development.

Forgiveness

Are you highlighted here? Forgiveness leads us to pray for those whose thoughts and principles mesh with our own. Then, there are those whose information we clearly process with an obvious lack of wisdom and understanding. The capacity to nurture wisdom on some days honestly escapes all of us. Thus, each of us becomes a member of another's list of people needing an extra measure of grace.

IT'S SIMPLY A BLUR

od's favor shines through my years of employment, from my very first job as a dishwasher to other professional positions waiting in the shadows. I come from a line of life models that considered getting a good-paying job the primary goal in life. There was little grooming

> And the God of all grace, who called you to his eternal glory in Christ, after you have suffered a little while will himself restore you and make you strong, firm and steadfast. To him be the power for ever and ever. Amen
> **1 Peter 5:10–11 (NIV)**

for or discussions about a career. Absolutely no discussions about being happy in the moments that I was living. Family planning or marriage was not discussed in my home setting or any High School classes. Oh, yeah, there once was a statement from one older female who I lived with at one time, "if you ever see a red stain in your underwear, let me know." Beginning and end of discussion. I mean, this was the complete extent of my feminine education about my body. My male-female relationship discussion was like this — "Don't ever let a man or any older boy touch your private parts. They are never up to any good." My look back cannot ignore how this great blanket of protection was pure, empty nonsense. But at those painful growth moments, while crisscrossing adulthood amongst my private Forest called life, favored, or blessed by God, certainly did not dominate my primary emotions. I simply didn't know how to grab hold of the easy opportunities meant to be helpful. Here I was, in a state of confusion about relationships like those with my family unit and those beckoning for intimacy. What's love? How do I know whom to trust when my life is still full of mixed messaging about the definition of a prosperous future? Mixed messages about my value as a human.

My upbringing armed me with a satchel full of proof that tagged me socially naïve. Off I sprang into a world of assorted adults, some with malicious intent; some wanting to be helpful. A flash back to high school days features Aunt Jasmine being aw-struck with a neighborhood classmate because she had fair skin and shoulder length black hair. This classmate embodied my aunt's ideal features for an ideal girly appearance. In hindsight, Aunt Jasmine's assessment reflects what her family had handed down to her. We were all products of the deep south; shaped by majority definitions of beauty. Therefore, according to her analysis, my features, kinky hair, and a darker skin tone would hold me back. These traits helped to classify me as unpleasant to the natural eye. "Look at this lipstick," Aunt Jasmine's voice squeaked, as she came into the dining room wearing my pink lip gloss, "just look at this mess, she continued to say to anyone who happened to be in the dining room. Why would dark skin Meka choose this color?" All my cousins and uncle gathered around the table, smiled, and giggled in agreement. I ran outside in tears, feeling humiliated and misunderstood. To this day, it's tough to wear light colors on my lips.

Then there were those unspoken features about Mama hiding amongst the trees in my forest too. One instance that comes to mine happened during my late teen years. I can still see myself, standing in the doorway on the freshly painted gray wooden porch of a white house. It's the conclusion of a visit with my stepfather's family. Their comforting words were, "I know many people didn't like your mother, but we did. Regardless of what you hear, we thought she was a wonderful mother."

Core maternal family members said I would never amount to very much because I was my mother's daughter. I never understood exactly what the "just like your mother" statement suggested. But I heard it often enough from core maternal adult family members to keep it plastered up front in my thoughts as a negative feature. Remember, Mama died when I was nine years old. What was their role in shaping me over these later years of my development?

My social skills were limited to what I learned at my Baptist Church during my preteen years until high school. Things like, "Our loving God is a punisher of those who get caught-up in sin. Particularly stealing, sassing adults, and fornication!" No acknowledgement of God being loving and forgiving in my childhood settings.

Living the reality of a budding profession with the hospital continued unfolding and moved me from the tray-room to becoming a medical lab helper. Enrolling at the Community College was paying off. Soon after graduating with an applied science associate degree, I made plans to attend a four-year school while continuing employment.

My grades remained above average, even without me fully applying the required study time to my academic rigor. There were parties to host and more than enough ways to explore my new freedom living in my first apartment. Qualifying for this upstairs one-bedroom unit was a great ego booster. Got it all on my own without a co-signer! This is about the same time I learned I was expecting my first child. It had only been a couple of months before this realization when Dr. Klopp had offered to give me a birth control prescription. But being too embarrassed to admit my hidden sin, I simply didn't know how to accept his help. I convinced him that my abstinence lifestyle was still successful. After all, I was working for a Catholic Hospital. Engaging in sex outside of marriage was a sinful abomination in my Baptist upbringing, too. During my pregnancy, these were two soul-piercing social incidents.

Over the years, a personal understanding of social norms, networking and asking for help would have leaps and bounds and hurdles to conquer. Work ethics were always on point. My boss and other hospital staffers showed their commitment and care by naming me the employee of the month early in my pregnancy. This recognition included an in-person chat with the hospital president, Sister Mary Frances. The manager of the hospital lab arranged the event, so it was a threesome. When Sister Mary noticed and mentioned … "You look like you're going to become a mom." The lab manager was quick to respond in a way that made it seem as if I was married. "She had better be," Sister Mary responded, and she continued, "No sex should happen outside of marriage, right?" Each of us smiled and nodded in the affirmative as the brief conversation turned to another subject. By this time, my life's experiences came with many challenging situations. My commitment to work and church allowed me to stay afloat through it all. I had female roommates, but for most of the emotional part of this prenatal journey, I felt depressed and isolated. Yes, the father of my unborn child was close by. He lived as near as across the street with his mother, father, and siblings. He was three years older than me but still hadn't been progressively sorting out his own career path. We all attended the same Baptist Church. But his family and I didn't have a relationship inside or outside of church. Having a grandchild on the way wasn't even a reason for them to reach out to me to bond. I wanted my son's father to care enough to do what was proper regarding our child. That character trait never materialized. As his plans to move on became clear, I felt no obligation to include this rogue father in my world of needs during or after pregnancy. There was no pressure on him from me for legal child support, and I detested any thought of government public help. Accepting handouts over my lifetime seemed to come with shameful strings attached. Strings that could give the gift bearer free rein in my personal space. I had a place to live, a job but not a car, yet. But by local standards, our household was in an excellent position. Even without a father or husband.

Another troubling happenstance during my pregnancy was the passing of the great Auntie I lived with four years immediately after mama's death. This is the same Auntie who made space for my mother in her home when mama ran away. Remember, mama left her adoptive parents in Alabama and returned to Mississippi with no place to live. Making the trip home for Auntie's funeral was very important to me. I expressed my deep yearning about attending the funeral with my paternal family. The wisdom of those with whom I had lived until graduating from high school was of utmost importance and pivotal. The advice offered by these elderly members of my valued family system startled me. "Just put a ring on your finger and come to the funeral. No one will know the difference." I thought to myself, "but I will know the difference." Their guidelines for my attending the funeral were not acceptable.

> You cannot travel back in time to fix your mistakes, but you can learn from them and forgive yourself for not knowing better.
> —Leon Brown

Both incidents, the hospital president's chat, and my great auntie's funeral, kept my social satchel filled to the brim with thoughts of being too tarnished to be included in mainstream society. Regardless of how I felt about my professional progression, the social label affixed to my forehead remained unchanged. My patchwork of a childhood emotional tapestry and now my own added social woes kept the feeling of shame front and center. This nurtured my early childhood feelings of imperfection.

After giving birth to a healthy baby boy, returning to my medical lab assistant's job was non-eventful. I remained a grateful Mississippi born and bred Baptist Christian. Thus, always carrying the burden of not being fully forgiven by God and also feeling as though taking the position of second best was a weighty obligation. And, remaining silent while the important people opined about matters that affected me never set well in my spirit. This always did and still makes me feel angry with myself. But as Leon Brown's quote reminds us, we cannot travel back in time to redo the past. Now, this work of forgiveness helps me praise God and forgive myself and others. Healing is in the air! It has proven to be a companion of the work of forgiveness.

Hiring a dependable babysitter was a critical next step. Then buying a reliable car and finding time to work on my Bachelor of Science degree. A professional opportunity with the local food company fell into my lap as a lab technician position. After a successful interview, they awarded the position in the research and development department to me. My assignment was testing products for vitamins. Oh, I really loved being in the lab prepping samples, preparing test solutions, and interpreting the results. This position made me feel important. They included my lab results in final reports. Friends and family heard a lot about my work. I was so proud of the scientific insight I was gaining about food. I made a decent salary, too. This kept our (my son and I) household running smoothly.

Friends drawn to me through informal social gatherings showed they were interested in my progress. Now, getting affirmation from my northern Mississippi folks, was still another evasive can-of-worms. I learned about their jeers and sneers from a paternal cousin who had recently moved to the mid-west. "You know those cases of treats you've been sending home for Christmas? Well, Aunt Jasmine and everybody in that house make jokes about it and call it a weird thing to give somebody. And, whenever you ask her to make you an outfit, rather than cut and size it like the pattern, she intentionally makes it larger, saying that you probably need it bigger than you are asking for with the pattern. Last time she saw you, you were bigger than this size."

This feedback from a trusted source left me devastated as I perceived the report to be trustworthy. It was believable because it fit the narrative I had heard all my life. I was never good enough. So, based on this insider information, I stopped sending the Christmas box offered by my company. Later, in a conversation some months following the Christmas season, Aunt Jasmine said, "You didn't send a treat box this Christmas. I missed getting it."

A stint in microbiology anchored my exposure to research and development. Working at the food company's research and development lab lasted twenty-five years. It wetted my love of travel. Visiting other food plants to facilitate new product startups was a trip I enjoyed, and I looked forward to, too. A project management leadership work style and a love for research blossomed during my employment with this company.

Employment there motivated me to complete my next two

degrees: Bachelor's and Master of Management. Completing my undergraduate degree is when exposure to "Maslow's Hierarchy of Needs" become a beckoning call to my psyche. His Hierarchy motivated me at both my studies for a Masters and later for my professional level degree. The model gave me something to shoot for. There hadn't been long term goal setting in my life. Now, there were elements that gave definition to life which might shape actions to move above the deficiency needs area. I often wondered if my sons and I would ever see life above the lower half of Maslow's triangle.

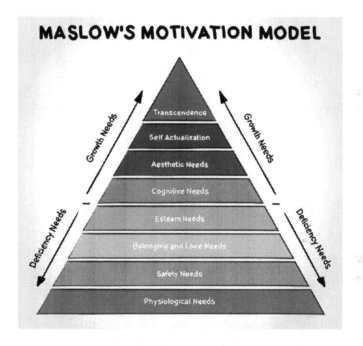

My core family still sneered, providing a backdrop for a life of long-term shame. By now, science intrigued me and a desire to learn more. My first option was to continue pursuing a degree in Food Science at a University near Detroit, Michigan. One semester toward that goal was all I could achieve. Maintaining full-time employment in western Michigan was a must. Since a food science degree required a four-hour round-trip drive and required both lecture and lab class sessions; it was impossible for me at that time. These requirements didn't fit well with my single parent status and responsibilities. Lord have mercy; Christ have mercy. Grace and gratitude can be spiritual forces that propel us ahead. Learn to call on spiritual forces for personal guidance, just as one does when [4]

- The sound of EMS vehicles prompts prayer.
- Seeing a school bus prompts prayers for kids.
- Consuming the daily news brings prompts for prayer.

My social life and personal choices continued to sputter. Never gaining enough altitude to take off and fly. I did eventually marry. Over time, several individuals to be blunt. Unfortunately, none with in-depth commitment or the capacity to provide for a family.

Forgiveness

We must strive to unpack our spiritual luggage, release clutter, and draw nearer to God.

Here are techniques I've tried for attitude adjustments. Daily affirmations help us express gratitude.

- I am appreciative.
- I am becoming more conscious of my surroundings and God's presence in each moment.
- I am blessed.
- Every day is an opportunity to make a difference.
- Every day is an opportunity to express the love of God.
- What would you add …?

---

[4] **The Gratitude Power Workbook: Transform Fear into Forgiveness, Isolation into Belonging** (2011) by Nina Lesowitz and Mary Beth Sammons

NOT IDEAL

For whoever finds me finds life and receives favor from
the Lord. But whoever fails to find me harms himself;
all who hate me love death. Proverbs 8:35–36 (NIV)

Allowing my brain to reflect on my past and edging toward
cultivating the lessons is moving my personal forgiveness
process forward. *The Rewired Brain* (Chilton, Rukstalis,
Gregory) described the human brain as the source of millions of
unconscious thoughts. Categorized as System 1 and far fewer conscious
thoughts System 2, sensations like desire, anger, fear, anxiety, hurt,
and unworthiness run in high gear in those whose trauma has not
been processed. When System 1 is working in overdrive, responses
happen quickly, without benefit of fact checking offered by System
2. This creates a path for an emotionally dysfunctional child to grow
into an emotionally dysfunctional adult. Our dysfunctions become
coping mechanisms, hoping to gain acceptance and avoid the pain
of rejection.

Becoming a single parent was not a wise or ideal choice, but it
certainly echoed the outcome of my social preparedness and naivety.
Why didn't I say yes to Dr. Klopp's offer or simply say "NO! Stop!"
to my partner? Maybe I thought he would like me even more.

I drifted through this single parenthood phase of life by rallying
my outer motions to match the rhetoric of my small "up north"
network of carefree buddies. On sunny afternoons, I saw them riding

around the neighborhood in a friend's black shiny Buick Regal convertible —

"Hey Meka," someone yelled from the back seat. "Want a ride?"

"No, I enjoy walking. It's excellent exercise for me."

"Okay. Someone in the car complimented, "You're taking good care of yourself." Their words only reflected what their human eyes could see rather than the darkness casting a shadow on my heart.

The required preparation for a child made the daily grind stressful. I melted inside with each jab from my southern family. Their deep-rooted principles about how best to please God and honor them haunted me in my pending unwed motherhood role. My teen years included regular church attendance and adhering to teachings from my elders about God punishing those guilty of sin. Perfection, without exception, was the golden rule by their standards.

A serious stage of tooth decay was well on the way by the time someone at my job asked me about my prenatal care. My medical insurance covered proper pre-natal care and other resources needed. My top priorities included working, building a nest-egg for those days needed for childbirth and maternity leave, and restructuring what had been a carefree single lifestyle. Then a slush of emotions centered on my baby's father and feeling set-aside made the journey to parenthood a heavy load. My mom's brief life as a wife and a victim of domestic abuse flashed before me. During her last pregnancy and other times too, my stepfather slapped her in the face and pushed her around many times. No way did I want that to be my epithet. *"If my partner will not step into his provider role without being pressured through the legal system, forget him, I'm done with him. He's not wanted here. Easy mindset to proclaim but difficult to live into. This is his child, too!"* This statement whirled on a repeat loop in my head. His nonchalant response broke my heart. I felt rejected by him, his family, and my own friends and family. Norms learned from my small-town upbringing were pressing my psyche.

I remembered my present condition was a disgrace during my high school years. Public scrutiny forced families to shield pregnant girls from public view. The movers and shakers treated unwed mothers as societal discards. My family projected their disapproval in me with comments like, "You're just like your mother." Mama wasn't married to my father.

But they affixed this negative "Mama" label to me from the time I was age nine; many years before becoming an adult. Many years before, I knew where babies came from. My maternal grandmother (Nana) wasn't married to my mother's father, either. It was Nana's choice to give my mother away after she finally got married. What a sad set of family conditions. No one thought it important to pass on their wisdom to rather than instilling feelings of embarrassment and mockery.

My personal vow to close the door on any parental rights granted to a father by the State of Michigan was vindictive but justified. Regrettably, he seemed okay with this approach. His absence didn't cause me any visible grief in those moments. I experienced no established model of fathering throughout my childhood. Yet I knew unfettered examples featuring a woman fighting through the obstacles of life with zero core family support.

Mama exemplified strength and courage in the face of challenge while married to an alcoholic who couldn't hold down a job. But a boatload of criticism seemed to inspire her to dream of a better life. She talked about moving to Alabama after giving childbirth to provide a better life for us. This mother of seven, including twins she gave up her life for, died in childbirth at twenty-eight. Oh, how deserted and abandoned she must have felt when her own mother denied her the bond of family love and approval. Had I become my mother? I am brought to tears for the both of us.

After my son was born, personal responsibilities expanded to include a babysitter, reliable transportation, stable housing, and a job. Once again, without panic or ever losing a spiritual beat, my entire list of basic needs seemed to align without undue stress. God's invisible hand had once again brought to bear all that we needed to survive and thrive.

My son's first babysitter, Sarah, was a caring middle-aged lady with four children aged four to thirteen. Her life circumstances made it necessary for her to accept public welfare. Sarah depended on me from time to time to pick up items for her children. One year, as we were all prepared for Christmas, she needed a ride to the Salvation Army's Gifts for Children Program. She scheduled this important ride with me. Remembering my tendency to be tardy:

"Meka, I need to pick up these gifts within my allotted time. Can you make it here to give me a ride to the appointment?" My babysitter asked a couple of days ahead of her appointment.

"Yes, no problem. I'll give you a ride."

She contacted me again within 20 minutes of her scheduled time. "Are you sure you can get me there on time? Lacey is here and he can take me. My kids won't have Christmas gifts if I miss my time slot," she reminded me.

"Yes, I'm leaving my house now."

Despite my best efforts to be on time, we arrived late, and the Salvation Army giveaway was over. They had locked the doors. Injuring the well-being of Sarah and her family caused a profound, dark feeling within me. I made a stab at purchasing Christmas items for her children. My pockets weren't deep enough. Plus, my lack of respect and sensitivity for another's concerns signaled what I had not recognized, in those moments, how I was being too inwardly focused. I seemed to really live in a woe is me mentality. Couldn't see the forest for the trees, nor was I able to drink from the river of life that flooded my daily presence.

I've never been a violent person when I felt stressed. My painful personal woes made me act out my bitterness in subtle ways. Saying things like "I feel depressed" during a meeting would often draw limited attention my way. I showed my need for care and acceptance by arguing and accusing others.

My conservative Mississippi upbringing continued to frame my interaction with males who stepped into my dating circle. There was no agreeing on sexual intimacy without first making a long-term commitment that led to marriage. By the time my son turned one and a half, I was married and the owner of my first home. My husband was tall and slimly built. He sang in a local five-member pop group with his brothers and two friends. Impersonating the Motown Temptations, their performance bookings were at nightclubs in the surrounding area. Our holy matrimony caved from the weight of me being the only gainfully employed partner.

My husband carried Sickle Cell Anemia and often needed to be hospitalized for blood transfusions and leg ulcers. No children were born during this union. His family was always lukewarm about our marriage because I had a child. They felt he could do much better in choosing a mate. We lived through three years of disagreements about money and lack of respect. After our divorce, he passed away. I attended his funeral services, which were hosted at the neighborhood church we all attended. During the public viewing, I said hello to one of his brothers and asked,

"Do you remember me?"

"No, should I?"

"No, not really," as I made a rigid pivot, turning my back to him walking away, feeling ashamed and deep embarrassment.

Another family member must have been in earshot of our brief exchange and told him who I was because he attempted to engage me in small talk later as I was leaving.

There were two more serious relationships and two more marriages. One at a time, of course, and an upgraded home. My next heart throb was a gainfully employed Vietnam veteran with a cheery personality and fun to be around. We enjoyed teaming up at house parties and nightclubbing. His factory job paid well, but taking time off work was a regular occurrence. He often stayed out late gambling with his friends. Then, his second talent next to gambling was seeking ways to qualify for sick leave. Two years into our marriage, as my oldest son turned eight years old, I was expecting my second child as planned.

We shared the same circle of friends who also had a son close to the age of my oldest son. We were both rebounding from a first marriage and thoroughly seemed to enjoy each other's friendship. He had three children from his previous marriage, and an ex-wife that dragged him to child-support court regularly because he missed work and would not make his required payments.

His mother and stepfather lived in the same neighborhood as we did. They treated me and my first child nicely. When labor pains started, my husband's knee surgery had him hospitalized, so my in-laws went to the hospital with me. The birth of my second son was a long, painful ordeal. Birth pains were a small price to pay for the joy of a second child. This time, within the bounds of holy matrimony, just like society says, it should be done.

During this moment of happiness, I learned my husband had been unfaithful during our marriage. Bottom line, I wasn't the only one carrying a child he had fathered. After being discharged from the hospital, he lived with his mother and stepfather. We never lived together again after our son's birth. This time, I insisted on child support and the deed to our family home as part of the divorce settlement. His parents and siblings always recognized our son, as well as the other children fathered by my ex-husband. He became inconsistent with his court approved parenting visitation schedule and child support. Three years later, he married a third time and had two more children. He would later pass away. Our son was old enough to be present at his father's funeral without my participation.

Within five years later, my next marriage developed from a causal relationship that moved to weekend sleepovers. My friend and his family were nice to both of my sons. They always included us in their family reunions in Florida during the summers. Our relationship blossomed, despite an underlying family trait of abusiveness toward women. This core family consisted of a father, stepmother, three brothers, and a sister, all adults living productive lives and maintaining regular jobs. My employment with the food company was going well, too. My friend and I got married during the second year of our relationship. By this time, both of my sons would spend four to six weeks during the summer in Mississippi. He joined me for the round-trip drives to pick up the boys and stops in Tennessee's Great Smoky Mountains and amusement parks on our return to Michigan made these fun family trips.

Our marriage took an abrupt, serious turn for the worse when I accused him of cheating on me after I returned from one of my business trips. A blow to the top of my head with his fist accompanied his verbal response to my accusation. After I regained conscientiousness, he left the house. I called a relative in tears, pondering whether I should go to the hospital and contact the police. Within half an hour, my husband's father called to see how I was; a sign that my husband had retreated there. I later learned that he used my address book to reach-out to my female acquaintances to become girlfriends. Before this realization, I had considered them friends.

This marriage developed into a full fledge drama filled with domestic violence and abusive attacks. He began spending nights away from home. Then came the intimidation with his words and actions, such as gripping my neck and pressing me against the wall, pushing the barrel of his shotgun up my nostril. Then later leaning the gun against the wall next to our bed to intimidate me after kicking me out of our bedroom.

Infidelity on his part filled every nook and cranny of our existence as a couple. This seven and a half-year marriage ended in divorce, too. He passed away in recent years, but over time he expressed regrets about the way he misused my trust. No, we never attempted to reconcile. I always declined his overtures. There were no offspring from this union. We were never in each other's presence alone again.

My current marriage is a thirty plus year journey with someone who professes loyalty to God and worships the same Jesus who is dear to me. During this union, my quest for formal learning while considering my next professional move fueled my desire to be accepted by my husband and peers.

Business and personal travel both stimulate creativity and a sense of calming. Returning home after a trip was always a letdown. One such time when I returned home from a business trip, my husband met me at the airport. A comment I made to him triggered, "I don't work for you." At that moment, I heard the comment, but really didn't know what he meant or what he was reacting to. I let it go. He never followed up with a similar statement during our ride home.

What prompted that? I thought to myself. I let his statement drop to the car mats when he never offered further comments. Not even a partial explanation during our silent hour-long ride home.

But he actually clarified his words some days or even weeks later. We both wanted a glass of juice. He filled a glass, I said, "thank you." With a deep condescending tone while making eye contact, he yelled, "I didn't pour that for you!" I stepped back, somewhat shocked, and then got a glass for myself. I encountered other incidents of increasing disrespect in the following years. These attacks were an obvious source of verbal abuse. Given my track record, I was determined to make this marriage work.

Travel and time with this food company expanded my knowledge and also built my core mindset about teamwork and project management across various disciplines. Product start-ups and prototype development gave me exposure to team building. Nothing in my past encounters had pushed me toward thinking about a career rather than a well-paying job. But I was moving in that direction. I set my longer-term vision on a higher level of management, human resource development, or even a completely different career.

Honing my skills would better align with my longtime core interest in teaching. Since my middle school days, teaching appealed to me. But now the idea was shifting to teaching adults by developing a robust adult education program. A curriculum teaching leadership to entry level prospects piqued my interest. My job included hiring and even dismissing new hires during their probationary period. I hated firing people; however, this was a component of my job. After some pondering and consultation, I enrolled in the Educational Leadership Doctoral Program at Western Michigan University.

"At its highest level, forgiveness includes a willingness to consider that many causes and conditions, including pain or ignorance, can lead people to bad things. Enright's list of what forgiveness is not might make you think.[5]

[5] **The guide to Compassionate Assertiveness: How to Express Your Needs & Deal with Conflict While Keeping a Kind Heart** by Sherrie M. Vavrichek, LCSW-C

- Forgiveness is not glossing over wrongdoings, denying the seriousness of an offense, or pretending that things are different from the way they really are.
- Forgiveness is not excusing or condoning wrongdoing and does not remove appropriate consequences.
- Forgiveness is not denial or forgetting.
- Forgiveness is not an excuse to control other people.
- Forgiveness does not mean you have to trust the person.
- Forgiveness does not have to involve reconciliation.

Forgiveness

Here's a recommended list from Enright in Vavrichek's chapter entitled *Forgiveness: Free Yourself from Anger* that resonates with most of us. At this step of my journey, the last two items

- **Forgiveness does not mean you have to trust the person**.
- **Forgiveness does not have to involve reconciliation**.

> What connects most with you from this short list? Why?

PUSHING THROUGH

> So, throw all spoiled virtue and cancerous evil in the garbage. In simple humility, let our gardener, God, landscape you with the Word, making a salvation-garden of your life (The Message – James 1:21)

Theodis was in his mid-fifties, ten years my senior, when we said, "I do." We met in midwestern Michigan at church and continued our church-centered relationship after I moved to a neighboring town. Before the wide use of cell phones, it made sense for our marriage pact to include each of us keeping our established phone lines. Over time, I learned his factory buddies kept conversations going between their scheduled second shift work hours. After-work conversations were a significant use of his landline. He referred to those chats as spiritual counseling. It was common for a session to last more than a couple of hours.

Weeks later, I had an encounter at the entryway of our local Sam's Club. One Saturday morning, a male shopper and I worked to separate a few stuck carts before we could shop. We finally freed one, and a set of four remained. I reached for the single one - "I didn't do that for you," he said as he pushed the free cart toward the shopper's membership verification area.

No problem. I thought we were working together; I said to myself as I worked to separate another one from the remaining cart cluster.

Theodis was spending his off day at home and greeted me when I arrived from shopping. We chatted about the weather and the backyard flower garden as I unpacked bargains from Sam's Club. "A cold glass of iced tea would be good about now," I said.

"Yeah, that sounds good," he chirped while retrieving and filling a glass.

"Thank you."

"I didn't pour that for you!"

I was deeply shocked by the harsh roar of his voice. His white-knuckle grip on the glass made me resist the urge to yank it from his hand. But replaying and framing the similarity between my husband's response to me; the response I heard in my Sam's Club encounter, plus his airport greeting, were unavoidable. It made me relive the feelings of disrespect and humiliation from my earlier encounter. I had no connections to the guy at Sam's Club, so I only viewed him as an unkind, rude person. But hearing similar words out of my husband's mouth a second time felt like a punch in the gut.

I asked myself, "Is this what I've signed up for in years to come of married life —head throbs from emotional stabs and degrading shaming?"

I took a step back, pivoting toward the cabinet, away from his piercing glare, to get a glass. I poured myself tea and made a beeline to my home office with fumes of anger puffing from my nostrils.

Over time, Theodis became more of my nemesis than a partner investing in a healthy marriage. He thrived on creating countless moments, using irritating verbiage to rattle my spiritual balance. For over twenty-five years, his antics led me to respond in ways that exposed my inward turmoil through second guessing my decisions. My outward appearance of indecisiveness increased his church-wide favor, while it made those same folks question my agency. Disrespect became commonplace. For example – my job responsibilities would often require me to stay onsite after many functions to ensure that the building was locked and secured. Theodis would often leave me there, while making it a priority to give a female parishioner a ride home.

I never considered the benefit of having the support of a personal mental wellness counselor. I convinced myself Theodis' shenanigans were minor. At least, I thought so at the onset. My point of reference was the physical pain of domestic abuse I lived with until I escaped a previous marriage. Infidelity was a common thread among them, but domestic violence was another category of hurt. Abusers may make recipients feel that they're oversensitive. Many excuse the behavior.

Yes, I believe Theodis intentionally played my emotions like a fiddle. He knew I placed a priceless value on simple expressions of acceptance and care. The highs and lows of his denial increased my stress level and, later, would affect my health. But in those moments, I was determined to push through my daily shower of shame and harassment to make our marriage work. Over our thirty-five-plus year marriage, Theodis made one family trip with me to my Mississippi hometown. His presence alongside me at local social outings was mainly non-existent.

Even though all three of my ex's were deceased, acquaintances and core family still held on to me being in my fourth marriage, disregarding its longevity. When my brother David died, our marriage was approaching its silver anniversary. But Theodis met my expectations concerning my brother's funeral. He did not attend. The typical pattern forged over the years entailed making him aware of my plans for family events and telling him how long a trip would take. My youngest son, grandson, and I rode to Mississippi for David's funeral. There were never enough layers for my skin to elude the pain of navigating functions without my husband's companionship. In hindsight, years later, I questioned my mindset because there weren't examples of women in the family receiving this level of nurturing care and support. None had been treated as queens.

My brother's death led to my siblings, our maternal uncle, and me organizing our first family reunion. After our separation as young children by our grandmother, we all still lived in the same town until my high school graduation. But we hadn't made it a practice of being in touch. Why didn't senior family members encourage us to reach out to each other?

When my sister Mandy and I planned a one-on-one meetup during our first maternal family reunion, I entered the moment with the mentality of my nine-year-old self. In those days, we were all sad and confused about losing our mom and would soon experience the pain of our fragile sibling ties ripping apart. That's the time when tears flowed from five-year-old Mandy's eyes while asking me, "when are we going back home to live with Mama and Daddy?"

But in this moment of renewal after many years of separation, Mandy's burning direct questions for me were:

"What does it feel like to have been with so many men?" "How does a person do that?"

Mandy's inquiry was a complete surprise.

Why is she asking me something like this? I wondered.

My heart broke, piercing my soul. I did my best to respond to her inquiry without using the judgmental words tumbling around in my head while asking myself, *where does a God-fearing, God-loving individual find such a level of self-righteousness to cast stones at their family members? Isn't this supposed to be a relationship building for senior adults?* But unfortunately, none of my critics, family, or clergy associates ever called me with words of comfort, suggested counseling, or offered to hear my lived reality. No one cared that much!

While living in midwestern Michigan, Theodis never supported my local invitations to speak at churches or other functions in our beloved community. No complimentary comments toward me passed through his lips.

"I'm not taking on a cheerleader role for you," he often reminded me.

So, I didn't expect him to be in the audience or fulfill this vowed partner role with his presence. Having Theodis act as a confidant in chief in public, even if not at home, would have made me happy. In hindsight, he had his underground network of church associates, primarily women, tucked in his inner circle, enjoying his monetary gifts under the guise of benevolent offerings. Incidents like a onetime promise he claimed to have forgotten come to mind. Who knows …It could be an additional request made that very morning.

"Meka, I need $50 back from the money I gave you," he said one Sunday after worship as I left the pulpit. "I promised Julie help with food for her kids." I carried cash and gave him the total amount without discussion in those days. After all, we were in a public setting, and my all is well persona had to be maintained.

On another occasion, he brought a gift home. It was a cake from one of his church's female fanbase. I later learned who gave him the cake and made it my business to thank her for baking us a cake. The cake baker smiled sheepishly during our interaction. She later chastised him for asking her to bake a cake for us. Behind closed doors, I pitched a hissy fit and demanded, "never ever bring anything else into this house from any of your private bakers."

During my studies, we lived and worked in Michigan cities near Detroit. My committing to seminary full-time in 2004 would start our migration to Ohio. But unfortunately, married life had fewer and fewer hopeful moments. Alongside the blinding light of shameful hurt, there wasn't movement toward commitments to date night, taking part in couples' counseling, or even sharing a birthday meal at home …

"Happy Birthday, Theodis. I know you don't want to join me in dining out. Place a takeout order at Cracker Barrel, and I'll pick it up after my meeting at church."

"Okay, I will," Theodis nodded as I gave him my written order.

"The food is here," I called out to Theodis upstairs as I rounded the kitchen counter. I was sure he heard the garage door motor when I opened the door from his bedroom since it's over the garage. He came down, gathered his food, and headed back upstairs. When he was midway up,

"Aren't you going to stay down here and eat your birthday meal?"

"Oh, you want me to stay down here with you?"

"No, that's okay if you don't want to."

Eating meals alone was commonplace in our northern Ohio household. There were ongoing jabs about my quest for self-improvement. "You are always trying to be a big shot," Theodis would say. Perhaps he saw his neglect as punishment for my focus on achievement. In contrast, his free time focused on arguing with others about Scripture and increasing the participants on his pseudo-counseling line, especially damsels in distress.

He worked hard to stay connected with his female Michigan friends after he moved to Ohio. From time to time, I overheard him having long caring conversations with females. One time I clearly heard him say to a caller, "Sound like you need a man." He made many mailings to his female acquaintances like birthday and thinking of you cards with a token cash gift.

His interactions with East Ohio United Methodist parishioners and community members generated few new relationships, and these didn't strengthen our own. My marital woes made me decline attempts by my District Superintendent to appoint me to another congregation. Relationships are never perfect. Developing and working on a strategy for improvement is healthy. We never arrived at this milestone in our marriage.

My survival techniques gave way to rage behind closed doors while attempting to maintain a polite public demeanor toward him. His attacks weren't physical like other experiences, but they fell within a stress-inducing realm known as domestic verbal abuse. Verbal abuse isn't visible, but it has a negative effect on those who live with the experience.[6]

Mistreatment comes in different forms and from a variety of human interactions. It could be a threat of physical abuse, words, or actions that damage an individual's sense of well-being. Interfering with one's independence and emotional wellbeing falls into this category, too. I have often embraced the majority definition without ever sharing my story. I have neglected to grasp the expanded

---

[6] https://www.betterhelp.com/advice/abuse/would-you-recognize-verbal-abuse-heres-what-you-need-to-know/

definitions of domestic abuse and suppressed its inclusion of family dynamics, which leave scars and periods of low self-esteem, and it can weaken one's self-confidence. The stress level of my unhealthy home environment manifested itself through my personal physical health. I have learned to recognize the years of busyness as meaningful, but also as my coping mechanism. It was during my final two years in Ohio that my doctor diagnosed me with type 2 diabetes, non-Hodgkin lymphoma and then pneumonia in one lung. The lackluster support received, and questionable home care made it necessary for me to make permanent changes.

Surviving without thriving kept my pastoral cup below half full. As the adage says, "we can't pour from an empty cup" (John Fleming). A triggering health event in my later years brought my closed-door reality full circle. I asked myself what there is about some of us that seem to pull us toward partners who cannot be supportive and unwilling to seek healthiness in relations.

Professor Elaine Johannes[1] defines verbal abuse to include tactics to instill fear of humiliation, failure, physical violence, or abandonment. Abusers can be parents and romantic partners. I have observed abusive traits among casual acquaintances, too. Dr. Johannes' explanation takes me back to acts of childhood shaming, where adult caretakers help mold my brain to see myself as the lesser.

Emotional clutter paralyzes; emotional clutter can harm more than our relationships with friends, family, and co-workers. Our relationship with God can suffer too. Oswald Chambers was an early twentieth century Scottish Baptist evangelist and teacher. He wrote, "It is incredible what enormous power there is in simple things to distract our attention away from God." (Oswald Chambers, My Utmost for His Highest [Grand Rapids, MI: Discovery House Publishers, 1992], Nov. 23)

Forgiveness

Every time you feel hurt, offended, or rejected, you have to dare to say to yourself: "These feelings, strong as they may be, are not telling me the truth about myself. The truth, even though I cannot feel it right now, is that I am the chosen child of God, precious in God's eyes, called the Beloved from all eternity, and held safe in an everlasting embrace." Henri J. M. Nouwen

> A clean conscience is a soft pillow
> — German Proverb

PESKY RELATIONS

The LORD is my light and my salvation—
whom shall I fear?
The LORD is the stronghold of my life—
of whom shall I be afraid?
2 When the wicked advance against me
to devour[a] me,
it is my enemies and my foes
who will stumble and fall.
3 Though an army besiege me,
my heart will not fear;
though war break out against me,
even then I will be confident.
4 One thing I ask from the LORD,
this only do I seek:
that I may dwell in the house of the LORD
all the days of my life,
to gaze on the beauty of the LORD
and to seek him in his temple.
5 For in the day of trouble
he will keep me safe in his dwelling;
he will hide me in the shelter of his sacred tent
and set me high upon a rock.
6 Then my head will be exalted
above the enemies who surround me;
at his sacred tent I will sacrifice with shouts of joy;
I will sing and make music to the LORD.
7 Hear my voice when I call, LORD;
be merciful to me and answer me.

8 My heart says of you, "Seek his face!"
Your face, LORD, I will seek.
9 Do not hide your face from me,
do not turn your servant away in anger;
you have been my helper.
Do not reject me or forsake me,
God my Savior.
10 Though my father and mother forsake me,
the LORD will receive me.
11 Teach me your way, LORD;
lead me in a straight path
because of my oppressors.
12 Do not turn me over to the desire of my foes,
for false witnesses rise up against me,
spouting malicious accusations.
13 I remain confident of this:
I will see the goodness of the LORD
in the land of the living.
14 Wait for the LORD;
be strong and take heart
and wait for the LORD.

Psalm 27

Pain can sometimes make you selfish. After over 40 years since this personal experience, I feel compelled to add my voice to those speaking to keep domestic abuse top of mind as a societal issue. Globally, this kind of abuse is behavior acted out by both males and female. It is a need to hold dominance and authority over the one subjected to the abuse. A threat to do physical violence could be the reason for it. It might come as harsh words or actions that damage a person's sense of independence and emotional well-being. Most decision makers agree that the behavior results in gender specific injury.

> Defined by the Ananias Foundation: Domestic abuse is when one person mistreats another who is part of their household, family, or is in a dating or marriage relationship with them. A domestic abuse definition can include mistreatment of an older family member (elder abuse) or a child (child abuse) or hurting our intimate partners.

I have experienced most of the domestic abuse definitions in past years without sharing personal knowledge about any part of it during my own expressions of helping others heal in my role as a pastor. I neglected to speak into the consequences of domestic abuse and thus suppressed its inclusion in the analysis of family dynamics that have left scars and contributed to stints of low self-esteem, self-doubt, and a lack of confidence.

Yes, my life's journey has encountered abusers that acted out domestic abuse definitions. There was a time when I have undergone physical violence. I truthfully lived in fear. Like so many others, I did not press charges, even after taking a violent blow to the back of my head that left me unconscious for a short time. Other abusive behavior during that relationship made me feel trapped when my husband pushed the barrel of a gun in my right nostril to quiet my reaction to his violent behavior. Then he threw me out of our bedroom. The shotgun that he placed next to the bed became a symbol of intimidation and a reminder of the newly established bedroom rules. My types of abuse include physically battered, intimidated, and emotionally scarred.

The time came when I locked him out of the house and moved forward with a divorce. It is only by the grace of God that this man did not literally rip the back screen door off its hinges as I shared my intentions, standing just on the other side of this unsecured screen door. He chose not to retaliate in any harmful manner then or later as I moved forward with our divorce. I so clearly remember the day I arrived at court feeling alone and empty inside. As I left the courtroom chambers, my sad face triggered a stranger in the lobby to say hello. Then quickly mentioned the painful countenance I wore and wished me well as I walked hurriedly through the lobby. The divorce was a release from physical abuse, but its mental scars needed care that has been a long time coming.

In my later years, I hope that sharing this will help free up positive space in my personal karma to see me. I will continue asking myself why some of us pull from a pool of partners who cannot be supportive and unwilling to seek healthiness in relations.

The harm associated with domestic abuse manifests in different forms. It can prompt childhood experiences and feelings by actions or images occurring years later during adulthood; especially if there are unresolved sources of pain and hurt. Sharing life stories that reflect the viewpoint derived by a child who has spent her early childhood in spaces cultivated by an adult that lacked gestures of acceptance, like hugs and encouraging words, would be therapeutic. Some of my caregivers would say to me …

> ## "I'm doing more for you than your mama did!"

Perhaps adults providing my basic early childhood oversight and care were themselves conditioned by hurts and challenges rather than validation.

Reflection/Prayer

Lord, teach us! Teach us to manage the wrecking ball that follows us around. The swinging jabs that create openings to leash out blame at any perceived perpetrator. We call on your goodness to overcome our unwelcome attitudes.

CHURCH AND ME

I was young and now I am old, yet I have never seen the
righteous forsaken or their children begging *for* bread. They are
always generous and lend freely, their children will be blessed.
Psalm 37: 25-26 (NIV)

Sustaining active alignment with church became important
to me after Mama's death. Our family never attended the
neighborhood Baptist church while she was alive. Our rented
room was less than half a block from it. During my teen years, my
housing changed from Auntie Carrie Lou's home on Sixth Avenue
to Aunt Jasmine's home on Tenth Avenue. However, the church I
attended remained a steady influence. Now, in adulthood, it became
the centerpiece for keeping my spiritual development a priority.

As my sons grew older and were off at college or simply no longer
at home, my life became more one dimensional. Church was my only
social outlet, which limited my network. I found refuge by engaging
above and beyond expectations at work and school. Outreach and
assisting others from my ever-thundering home cultivated storm kept
me somewhat sane. Was it too much for God to grant me a marriage
partner who showed loving support?

Core Baptist teachings shaped all my tenets of faith. They
grounded my fearful respect for an angry God and what it meant to
be Christian. Going to Michigan from Mississippi right after high
school and connecting to a church like my childhood church was a

simple decision. My northern relatives showed their approval of this Baptist church too by attending it and providing financial help. No further discussion needed.

Our Independent Baptist fire and brimstone dogma taught about a God who favored an obedient, perfect individual. Independent Baptist teachings were uncompromising and intolerant of any flaws. Fear is used to ensure obedience. Our trusted self-governing church leaders defined acceptable Christian behavior in compliance with church doctrine passed down from one generation to another with no one seeking clarity. Defiance was always an option, but public shame and fear of authority kept us in check and mischief underground.

Teachings about a God of mercy and grace would come much later in my adult life. But the enraged God, as taught during my childhood and reinforced in early adulthood, slowly gave way to a more plausible theology.

A theology set to please an angry God kept me and historical family flaws behind the eight ball. Dutiful church work didn't remove the shame or silence of the religious church naysayers. The loudest negatively charged voices were still from down-home folks. But now those opinions were combined with a local mid-west Michigan unwed mother. She joined the chorus of critics and continues in that role.

Professional changes were ramping up at the same time I began experiencing another level of spiritual awakening. One sunny Sunday morning provided a unique experience for me. Everyone seemed emotionally engaged in singing and praying and praising God. The Pastor's voice was the next expected official sound with the 11 AM sermon. Standing in the soprano section of the choir loft, I clapped my hands to the rhythm of the praise song. Above all the competing joyous sounds of worship, a voice called out to me ...

"Tell them you're gonna preach."

Startled by what I heard, I immediately sat down. In the inner quiet of that personal moment, the voice spoke again ...

"Stand up and tell them you are called to preach."

Certain I was mistaken by what I heard, I declined to obey

the urge to share it in that instance. We already knew Baptist teachings and women weren't called as preachers during those times. Acknowledging this spiritual assignment, from what I believed to be a higher power, took more than one spiritual encounter and about five years for me to accept. Followed by another five years of meetings with various church leaders before being publicly ordained as a minister by the pastor of my Independent Baptist Church. While I proudly wore the label, access to resources and public recognition never fully materialized. Men still successfully guarded the path to the pulpit. My trailblazer role did eventually open the door for several other women to acknowledge a similar call to serve in our church.

A clergy appointment as pastor of a United Methodist Church in northeast Ohio, while I was attending seminary, made my life exciting. But it raised the stakes regarding the importance of moving back to Michigan after completing the seminary degree. Which would be the better option for our empty nest household? It took some convincing and a constricted Michigan household budget, but my husband reluctantly caved and moved to Ohio. The church didn't own a parsonage but provided a small housing stipend. We lived in a two-bedroom apartment for six-months while house hunting; later settling on a newly constructed condominium ten-minutes from the church. Theodis's move to Ohio meant a chance to revamp our relationship as we learned about the new community, or so I thought.

My United Methodist congregation worshipped in a transitioning neighborhood in an Eastside Ohio neighborhood. Most parishioners with the capacity to give from their abundance of both resources and talents had left to join suburban churches before my arrival. Completing seminary studies and the learning curve in a cross-cultural appointment included challenges like—Coalescing worship styles—Engaging in many heated conversations on seminary campus about cross-racial appointments was constant. The United Methodist nor other mainstream denominations had data to glean from on this practice in 2004. Other nuances from my ground-breaking cross-cultural appointment included addressing established administrative duties; balancing seminary and active pastoral responsibilities and establishing community credibility.

The Church's Caucasian office manager felt the impact of my presence on her overall established authority, which included check writing, ministry approvals, etc. She started scheduling meetings with contractors and community power players before my scheduled 10 AM arrival at the office. We neutralized her strategy when I changed my schedule to match hers. It's worth noting that our relationship improved after this bumpy start in community service and worshipping together.

The posture of the United Methodist Church and its unwillingness to commit adequate resources both personnel and fiscal or leverage its authority to attract needed resources for an inner-city congregation left me in a quandary. Our declining congregation was successful in linking to and designing programs that brought needed resources to our struggling community. Cuyahoga County leaders helped resource the church's community-based academic support for suspended K-8 students, a Benefit Bank and Food Distribution Program. The attention from other core community leaders didn't cultivate bridges but competition from their stronger and better resourced organizations.

Driving between my Ohio home and my seminary for class, leading a church and learning the new community kept me in an "I can't slow down; I am responsible for everything" unhealthy mindset. Time to play or rest wasn't on my agenda. Especially when my husband joined me in Ohio and became more focused on developing his own niche. Replicating his Baptist church norms, rather than creating a collaborative ministry with me as pastor, was not on his agenda. Our old Michigan spousal demons were now thriving in Ohio. It didn't go well.

"We either make ourselves miserable, or

Emotional *Sobriety*: From Relationship Trauma to Resilience and Balance by Tian Dayton, Ph.D. – We either make ourselves miserable, or we make ourselves strong. The amount of work is the same.

– *Carlos Castaneda*

we make ourselves strong. The amount of work is the same." – *Carlos Castaneda*

Trauma prompted by abuse, neglect, or addiction, causes our bodies and minds to react with frightening behavior, hurt, or to be overwhelmed with more intense emotion than we can process and integrate. These responses interfere with the development of our emotional sobriety. We recognize how emotional trauma changes not only the mind and heart of a person, but the body as well; how living with chronic emotional pain affects what we now know to be our limbic system; how when the limbic system is affected, our ability to regulate our emotions is undermined; and why we can't "just get over it" when we have been affected by the repeated mobilization of our own fear/stress response. Emotions predate reason. Our emotional wiring, that is our limbic system, is in place from birth but our thinking wiring isn't in place until we're around twelve, and even then, we're only beginning to learn how to use it. Because of this discrepancy in development, young children cannot use their thinking to make sense of and regulate their emotional responses to life. Good emotional sobriety reflects a well-balanced limbic system. The limbic system is the mind/body system that governs our mood, emotional tone, appetite, and sleep cycles, to name just a few of its wide-ranging functions. Repeat painful experiences – over which we have no sense of control and from which we feel we cannot escape- can, over time, deregulate our limbic systems. This may undermine our capacity to self-regulate. Our early experiences lay down the neutral template from which we operate for the rest of our lives. (We never talked about feelings during my childhood).

Continuous learning is essential:

From **Daedalus and Icarus** - *Daedalus and Icarus* – Since Minos controlled the land and sea routes, *Daedalus* set to work to fabricate wings for himself and his young son *Icarus*. He tied feathers together, from smallest to largest so as to form an increasing surface. **Daedalus** is a brilliant inventor—the Thomas Edison of his day. ... Desperate to flee the island, **Daedalus** uses wax to build some wings for himself and his son **Icarus**. Daddy **Daedalus** warns his son to fly at a middle height: the seawater will dampen the wings and the sun will melt them. – Everything in moderation is emotional sobriety.

- Children learn the skills of self-regulation through a successful attachment and bond. It is also through this powerful, intimate bond they gain a sense of relationship, self, and eventually autonomy ... build a sense of self between *her*self and caregivers.
- Emotionally sober people value and maintain relationships. They recognize that a solid network of relationships is stabilizing for them, that they benefit from a sense of belonging with and to other people.
- Long-term studies attest to the benefits of a strong relationship network in such predictors as health, longevity, and an overall sense of well-being. Relationships balance our limbic. They also provide what Abraham Maslow highlighted in his famous hierarchy of needs as our basic human need for belonging (1987).

> To whom or what set of processes do you contribute your self-regulation?

TIGHTENING FRAGMENTS

I will forgive their wickedness and will remember
their sins no more. Hebrews 8:12 (NIV)

"Where do you see yourself in five years?", the interviewer asked during my bid on an internal departmental position while at the food company. Unfortunately, my lack of a convincing response foiled my ability to move to the next level in the interview process. Sadly, no one had ever asked me about personal plans beyond my current life's juggles.

For years, I met people who said, "You look and act like a teacher." I embraced those comments as an omen and set secondary school teaching as a professional goal. But now, my professional educator idea was more about grooming adults pursuing entry-level business opportunities rather than educating 7-12 grade students.

Product startups and prototype development for a food company with domestic and international plants exposed me to a successful team-building model. My required business travel was an inspirational experience. It recharged my battery. Returning was always clearly an energy zapper and mood changer. Using cross-disciplinary skill-set team members became a core leadership principle for me. It influenced my attitude about the value of team building and its role in a successful outcome.

I envisioned paving a career path to upper management with an emphasis on human resource development. Aligning my skills with my core interest in teaching felt right to me. Empowering those who labeled marginalized energized my inner self. Teaching has been a career of interest since my middle school days.

Grooming entry-level prospects for business protocol and leadership skills piqued my interest. My Doctoral Program focused on Human Resource Development and required a commitment to investing in the success of others. After completing a Master's in Management Degree at Nazareth College, the need to maintain the rigor of another academic challenge made me feel respected and engaged.

You may recall that Nana proudly displayed high school and college graduation pictures of my maternal aunts on top of it. This represented the success of my mother's sisters. Their silence was deafening after Mama's death. We didn't benefit from my aunties' wealth of experience. It never came to lighten the mental load of my siblings and me. This cog in my journey expands the depth and width of my forgiveness process. Revamping my career amongst all those whirling negative home-grown jabs was an act of godly intervention. I seemed to wear blinders while my heart ached for a morsel of godly wisdom from my elders.

A literal case of immaturity and brain fog prevented me from recognizing these positive career opportunities. Enrolling in graduate school was a good move because college student status was an approved identity. I felt pride in wearing it. This academic environment used merits to judge me without coloring it with my entry into its learning circle. No one focused on whether I was an unwed mother or an individual with multiple failed marriages. My advisor suggested a second master's in education would shore up a pending educational doctorate. Given my overall plan to learn adult curriculum development, I charted a path to bypass a second master's degree after passing the Graduate Record Examination.

Enrollment in the doctoral program was going well. My committee approved my dissertation project, which measured the impact of parents' behavior on a child's ability to learn. In addition, I took time off my regular job to conduct research at the local County Social Service Office. Learning to network with community-based organizations and get parent approval for data collection increased my awareness of the work provided by local nonprofits and their need for volunteers.

My dissertation research was eye-opening regarding the work of our church, too. We were one hundred percent inward focused. As fate would have it, the local Community Foundation recruited me to work as a donor relations officer during the research phase of my project. I accepted the new job and rebranded my professional career with a focus on community-based nonprofit organizations.

Community-based work with the foundation exposed philanthropy from a vantage point I had never considered or even knew existed. They taught us to give tithes and offerings to our church, but there was no mention of supporting outside organizations. Development Officer roles included creating advised funds or new funds for families to leave a legacy. We made it easy for donors at all income levels to support their community's growth through charitable giving at the foundation. Building conduits for charitable networking was quite like building relationships. Transitioning from my corporate job into the world of community foundations and other philanthropic organizations was vital to my thriving. Establishing an endowed scholarship fund for adults committed to careers in community service was a highlight of my transition into the world of nonprofits.

This reset brought another executive leadership opportunity with the government-funded Faith-based Leadership Institute. And ultimately, a relationship with the United Methodist Church. Even though I had vowed to be FINISHED with school after completing my doctorate; shifting from an Independent Baptist Church to leadership with the United Methodist meant another round of academic studies if I wanted to become United Methodist leadership. Consideration for becoming a United Methodist elder required a master's level theology degree before entering the process. My three-year stint in the seminary began when I was in my mid-fifties. After completing off-campus evening classes in cities surrounding my hometown, I became a full-time seminary student at the Methodist Theological School in Delaware, Ohio. This was my very first time living on a college campus. It was my way of trying to have one area of focus rather than being stretched between multiple priorities. Weekend drives home from Ohio to Michigan lasted one semester. Six months after my seminary year began in Ohio, my husband retired from his job in Michigan.

Seminary started my long journey toward learning that God, like any caring parent, had standards and expectations, but God wasn't always angry about my flaws. Instead, our Creator had always been loving, kind, and graceful. God only wants the very best for all of us.

There's a latent element of trauma linked to our experiences that creates a barrier between us and our ability to operate at full capacity. Bishop Tutu shares that *forgiveness* is the best form of self-interest. We need to give voice to the violations and acknowledge the pain—shameful fear can take center stage and paralyze us. Forgiveness starts our healing process.

Forgiveness

Don't Quit

When things go wrong as they sometimes will,
When the road you're trudging seems all up hill,
When the funds are low, and the debts are high.
And you want to smile, but you must sigh,
When care is pressing you down a bit,
Rest if you must, but don't quit.

Life is strange with its twists and turns
As every one of us sometimes learns
And many a failure comes about
When he might have won had he stuck it out;
Don't give up though the pace seems slow –
You may succeed with another blow.

Success is failure turned inside out –
The siler tint of the cloud of doubt,
And you never can tell just how close you are,
It may be near when it seems so far;
So stick to the fight when you're hardest hit –
It's when things seem worst that you must not quit.

For all the sad words of tongue or pen
The saddest are these: "It might have been!"

Encouraging words by John Greenleaf Whittier
(1807–1892)

PEOPLE OF ALL STRIPES FILL GOD'S WORLD

Finally, brothers and sisters, whatever is true, whatever is noble, whatever is right, whatever is pure, whatever is lovely, whatever is admirable—if anything is excellent or praiseworthy—think about such things.
—Philippians 4:8 (NIV)

motionally sober people value and maintain relationships. They recognize that a solid network of relationships is stabilizing for them, that they benefit from a sense of belonging with and to other people. **Emotional *Sobriety*:** From Relationship Trauma to Resilience and Balance by Tian Dayton, Ph.D.

We all experience pain … and for many of us, that pain equals trauma and becomes psychological for us. Creating a sense of belonging seems elusive to some of us. After years vested in crafting this memoir project, I've come to recognize the impact of shame used to control my childhood experiences, their disturbance and distress that upset my emotional system and spiritual equilibrium. So, I marvel at people who learned the skill of maintaining solid relationships across their lifespan. A fate I have yet to master. My unwanted shame identities are associated with the messages set in place by my core Mississippi family.

The Center for Attitudinal Healing makes us aware of research that supports a link between forgiveness and health. We've gradually uncovered and learned about the inconvenient awkwardness of carrying the weight and burden of unforgiveness. Using our inconvenient replica of unforgiveness, carrying a small rock in our pocket (Desmond Tutu) — we rehearsed what forgiveness is not … it is not weakness, or forgetting, injustice, easy or quick. Telling our story and naming the hurt grants forgiveness for renewing or releasing problematic relationships.

You have read my series of circumstances that chronicle my childhood. Studying the losses reported in other sources can help us process personal suffering, which can make us feel isolated. We want to cease the theft of our dignity while remembering suffering helps us learn. This occurs when we choose to entrust the things that burden us mentally and spiritually to the people God has placed in our lives as guides. Some of us become so callous, it takes other sources of pain and hurt to move us onto a path of proper care. BetterHelp.Com is a service I've embraced in my later years.

What's on your list of personal change makers? My work within a northeast Ohio community makes my list and led me to writing a spiritual memoir. At this writing, my list comprises my last employer, the United Methodist Church, and several community organizations that I partnered with in volunteer roles.

Volunteering with a top heavy politically inclined organization wasn't a service that immediately aligned with my childhood experiences or tightly fit with my professional journey, though it did provide magnificent learning. In hindsight, my lack of offline negotiating or a desire to do so, made it a tremendous challenge for a demeanor built on support centered on trust and ethnical merit.

You will recall I'm familiar with ministries that organize people wishing to provide food, clothing, and other essential items. Sharing has been an integral part of my life that has shaped my worldview for living an ethical life. After Mama's death, my childhood wardrobe was one hundred percent "hand-me-downs" through my high school years. During those years, I made a mental Pac with myself to never wear "hand-me-downs" or secondhand clothes once I was an adult with a job.

My first installment of a personal book about forgiveness pushes me to remember several of my paternal aunts, Auntie Jasmine, and Evette. My Aunt Jasmine always welcomed strangers or family members needing encouragement or a meal or a babysitter. She was the neighborhood's go-to person. The wife of a church deacon and a stay-at-home mom who expected the best from everyone she encountered. Her sister, Aunt Evette, had the same breadth for changing the landscape of her community while creating an opportunity for those around her to fully engage in the world around them.

Aunt Evette was the first among her sisters to learn how to drive. Thus, in her ability to get buy-in, she convinced her brother-in-law to let her sister get behind the wheel, after some years. Uncle Zack was a proud Driver's Education Teacher. I remember Aunt Evette's efforts to get her neighbors to vote. A high-risk volunteer proposition for a Mississippi resident in the 1950s.

Like most youngsters in my age group, my priorities focused more on who liked me and seeking acceptance rather than the important work of my auntie. She didn't receive accolades for all her community engagement and the effect it had. I wasn't fully aware of each moment's impact but remain grateful for my childhood and the inner compass it created that guides me to give others a hand-up. During my younger years, I was an active member of the NAACP's Young Adult Council while living in Michigan. As I look back, I can see that my Aunt Evette and my upbringing influenced me to become an activist, with the goal of making a difference.

Volunteering in Ohio caused me to revisit my family's community organizing; especially those geared to empower congregations. As I put pen to paper, I am asking God to grant me the grace of forgiveness. I am reminded of my Aunt March, who was mentally ill and had to be institutionalized during her adult life until she passed away. Wow!!! I've never visited this part of my history. Perhaps actually knowing more about my Aunt March's mental illness would have put me in a different place when dealing with difficulties in life. Especially when needing to distance people who betrayed my trust to misuse and abuse my kindness.

In 2014, the bond with my religious governing body fell apart. Conditions that led to the sale of the UMC facility that housed our community ministry were troubling. This transaction left me feeling spiritually crushed. Yes, it had been on the market for months; my leaders gave me the opportunity for a clergy appointment beyond my current district to another congregation. But I declined for reasons surrounding my home conditions and martial relational woes. I had understood our existing ministry home to be grandfathered with any potential sale of the facility. It wasn't. This gave primary place to a spirit of anger, feeling rejected and a justified sense of internal rage. A distant third emotion was this lingering desire to complete what I saw as my mission ministry in my clergy assignment. Through my anger, I embraced the pride of, "you can be angry with the church but just don't speak negatively about the Church in public. You don't want to be known as the complainer." My prideful approach to anger seemed justified. I remembered the unpleasant feelings when I would previously hear laity and clergy talk negatively about each other. I didn't want to succumb to that sinful fault while ignoring my bent-on anger. The damage caused to my soul and the internal suffering caused by the need to forgive, alongside my home situation, were beyond stressful. Almost paralyzing, hurtful pain.

Our 501c3, established during my time in Michigan, spanned the life of the Ohio church. It remained active with the Internal Revenue Service. So, as I transitioned, this 501c3 seemed like a natural path for me to embark upon and continue serving the community. We had done fantastic work with students suspended from school, but we could never land a grant sufficient to fully provide staff salaries and other needs of a small nonprofit. I even tried moving in with another United Methodist congregation and developing a partnership with a school in that community. I signed on as a volunteer reading support school staff; but things never developed between the church and the school. So, that idea dimly vanished as I entered my 70's. My one-woman mission to change local education and do good for struggling students found its context, for a moment, in the Ohio Reading Corps (AmeriCorps). Over the course of the first school term, I became seriously ill with–Pneumonia, Ketoacidosis, Atrial Fibrillation and was hospitalized November 2018. These immediate triggering events stemmed from a weakened immune system after a fourteen-month treatment for non-Hodgkin lymphoma starting April 2017. Coupled with stress at home and my volunteer position with a Community Police Commission, the need for a healthier lifestyle was beckoning me. A brief stay in the hospital re-ignited my 2016 conversation about moving closer to family.

The selection for the inaugural Community Police Commission September 2015 included me among the ten. The Community Police Commission (CPC) was organized in response to a federal mandate called a Consent Decree. Community ideas are considered for police policies to help strengthen the connection between officers and the people they serve. As Commissioners, we dedicated ourselves to studying our own City Council protocol and investigating protocol in cities with similar federal mandates in order to provide recommendations for policy updates. This new startup requires a use of personal resources and significant personal time.

These areas of cumulated stresses made life a challenging proposition when both internal and external clouds of dominance collided. A series of personality clashes would help usher in recruits for replacement chairs whenever a leader left. The leadership's strength waxed and waned with intensity, never completely fading away. Amid this unstable climate, the Commission created a staffing structure. Staff reflected the characteristics of the parent body. Yes, we added staffing issues to the existing malleable foundation, which was looking for a solid base. -it has not and probably did not happen. After serving two four years terms, it became clear spiritual wellbeing was not thriving. I must walk and serve in the strength of my calling. I was not compatible with the rigor and political ethos needed to be a successful commissioner. Being confident of this, he who began a good work in you will carry it on to completion until the day of Christ Jesus Philippians 1:6.

I'm grateful to God for guiding me away from bottled-up anger to the liberation of forgiveness. Lord, I thank you for the lesson I have learned at 71 years of age: I need to practice "self-forgiveness". It's critical for me to forgive myself every day.

"Therefore, since we are surrounded by such a great cloud of witnesses, let us throw off everything that hinders and the sin that so easily entangles, and let us run with perseverance the race marked out for us. Let us fix our eyes on Jesus, the author and perfecter of our faith, who for the joy set before him endured the cross, scorning its shame, and sat down at the right hand of the throne of God. Consider him who endured such opposition from sinful men, so that you will not grow weary and lose heart!" Hebrews 12:1-3 (NIV)

We find being judgmental and not forgiving at the root of unhappiness. Unhappiness keeps us clinging to the dark past, even when we long to be released. The Center for Attitudinal Healing makes us aware of research that supports a link between forgiveness and health. Deciding "not to forgive is deciding to suffer." Does The Center's findings suggest that forgiveness is a viable option for dealing with hardship? Anyone can learn forgiveness at any age, regardless of their current belief system; the past they have experienced, or the way they have treated others around them. The process of forgiveness wipes the slate of a painful past clean. Our attachment to unforgiveness hides the welcome sign to peace and happiness with anger. Forgiving others is the first step in forgiving ourselves (*Forgiveness: The Greatest Healer of All* by Gerald G. Jampolsky, M.D[7].).

---

[7] Dr. Gerald Jampolsky was a graduate of Stanford Medical School and a child and adult psychiatrist. He is the founder of the first Center for Attitudinal Healing in Sausalito, California

Forgiveness: (*A Course in Miracles* by Marianne Williamson)

- "If we have fearful or hurtful things that happen to us when we are young, we not only remember them, but we cling to them for judging the present and the future.
- Our minds are like motion-picture projectors. Our memories of the past become the images we project out onto a screen. And the screen for our projections is often whatever person we are talking with in that moment.
- The outcome is that our egos convince us that all our uncomfortable thoughts and feelings are caused by people or situations in the external world.

HERE AND NOW ...

There is now no condemnation for those who are in Christ Jesus, because through Christ Jesus, the law of the Spirit who gives life has set you free from the law of sin and death. Romans 8:1-2

> Long-term studies attest to the benefits of a strong relationship network in such predictors as health, longevity, and an overall sense of well-being. Relationships balance our limbic. They also provide what Abraham Maslow highlighted in his famous hierarchy of needs as our basic human need for belonging (1987). **Emotional *Sobriety*:** From Relationship Trauma to Resilience and Balance by Tian Dayton, Ph.D.

Yes, God placed me in those Independent Baptist Churches where learning to recite Scripture gave me the inner voice and inner comfort to persevere. Yes, the inner trumpet kept blasting, blasting, "you can get an education and you can get and keep a good job." Your alternative voice, your voice from your dark side, is the primary constraint to your outward mobility. By most statistics, I should not have made it to this point …I've made it this far by God's faithfulness and God's amazing GRACE! Lord, teach me to "forgive me." So, my four-fold portal (childhood, church, education, relationships) has a common thread—acceptance and pinned up anger for those who prey on my kindness.

We can take back control from negative influencers using "The Forgiveness Project: How's That Working for You?" Let me be clear! There are no victims here, only victors, when we commit to align our purpose with God's purpose. The first leg of my initiative started September 2018 in Ohio as a Book Club Launch…

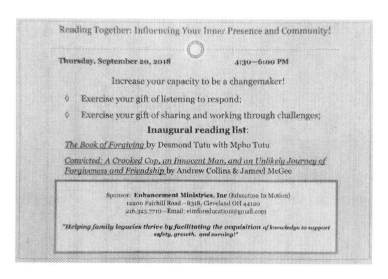

Face Book Live provided a platform to discuss what I was learning through readings other than Scripture and my volunteer services. I had managed my declining health, which was later associated with an enlarged spleen related to non-Hodgkin lymphoma by this time. Housing for my beloved nonprofit had traveled from four different places in Ohio. Now my repertoire of skills also included AmeriCorps as a classroom third grade reading support while maintaining my role with the Community Police Commission. Relational stresses at home were constant and internal home care was nonexistent through the fourteen-month treatment for non-Hodgkin lymphoma. At this time, I was unaware of being weeks away from my 2018 game changing hospitalization.

> Relationships balance our limbic. How are you seeking "balance?"

My spiritual journey started with a heavy heart set for prioritizing my health. As I wanted to make sure my relationship with God was in harmony, despite how people I had trusted were taking advantage of my kindness. Those who caused me immense heartache needed to be forgiven. Both past and current! I took a deep plunge into a theological river. This pushed the search of topics suitable for my Georgia podcast about how noble it is for "us" to model Jesus' actions and words associated with forgiveness. My intent provided fuel to explore the question of "How's that working for you?" served as As a guide to better speak about and understand forgiveness in action or practice. A tremendous refreshing undertaking, but not impossible with God's guidance.

As I waded through the forest, I discovered a shallow stream. It's fed by the river upstream. I encountered a stone there entitled—judgmental; then within a few more gentle drifts from that stone was another categorized as anger. At least three other stones bearing the words fear, perfectionism, and shame were among the tangible requirements. While gathering these stones, the spirit let me know, *"Meka, these are personal stones for you. While it's wonderful to champion forgiveness as a Christian discipline, remember charity starts at home."* We are not unhappy because we are unforgiving. We are unforgiving because we feel superior to others. Mercy is the fruit of the highest love, because love creates equals, and a greater love makes us inferior (*In Search of Beyond*, Carlo Carreto). Have you ever experienced a barrier to the greater love?

I humbly accept all my life's experiences and the learning God has sent my way. From childhood to adulthood, God has been my consistent companion – "All my life God has been faithful; His goodness is chasing after me! (CeCe Winans)". Relief and healing can be found amidst perfectionism, fear of shaming, and God's faithfulness. The deficiency needs area of Maslow's Hierarchy continues. Working alongside youth and teens in Ohio, besides my desire to continue ministry in the realm of forgiveness, set my heart to dancing at the cross of Jesus. I'm cherishing the rays of God's light for an abundant life. Yes, charity begins at home. Accepting my personal act of forgiveness remains an additional effort each day. Forgive thyself! And then show and share the act of forgiveness with those I encounter. God's grace makes a way for us to leave perfection in His hands. Learning to like and love myself in these recent years has given me a new purpose. Shedding tears of joy because of God's love for me and you are beyond comprehension.

Forgiveness

John 7 (NIV) After this, Jesus went around in Galilee. He did not want[a] to go about in Judea because the Jewish leaders there were looking for a way to kill him. ² But when the Jewish Festival of Tabernacles was near, ³ Jesus' brothers said to him, "Leave Galilee and go to Judea, so that your disciples there may see the works you do. ⁴ Since you are doing these things, show yourself to the world." ⁵ For even his own brothers did not believe in him.

> No one who wants to become a public figure act in secret. Go public with your stance. (THB)

ENDNOTES

1   Elaine Johannes is an associate professor and extension specialist in youth
    development in the Department of Applied Human Sciences at Kansas State
    University. Johannes has a bachelor's degree in psychology, a master's degree
    in adult and community counseling, and a doctorate in life-span human
    development from the School of Family Studies and Human Services at
    Kansas State University.

... from The Forgiveness Project

Thank You for Your Focus

God of presence, God our protector
God our provider!

Thank you for those you have placed before
us as faith leaders and spiritual discerners.

Grant a uniting of wisdom and a centering
on YOU!

In this season of enhanced social challenges,
Please give them words of healing, vision
and prophecy for your lands.

The Forgiveness Project
PYE Consulting Support

Printed in the United States
by Baker & Taylor Publisher Services